D0342724

MAR 1 6

AMERICAN FOODIE

AMERICAN FOODIE

Taste, Art, and the Cultural Revolution

Dwight Furrow

ROWMAN & LITTLEFIELD
Lanham • Boulder • New York • London

Published by Rowman & Littlefield
A wholly owned subsidiary of The Rowman & Littlefield Publishing Group, Inc.
4501 Forbes Boulevard, Suite 200, Lanham, Maryland 20706
www.rowman.com

Unit A, Whitacre Mews, 26-34 Stannary Street, London SE11 4AB

British Library Cataloguing in Publication Information Available

Library of Congress Cataloging-in-Publication Data

Furrow, Dwight, author.
American foodie : taste, art, and the cultural revolution / Dwight Furrow.
pages cm
Includes bibliographical references and index.
ISBN 978-1-4422-4929-5 (cloth : alk. paper) — ISBN 978-1-4422-4930-1 (electronic)
1. Food—United States—Philosophy. 2. Dinners and dining—United States. 3. Food preferences—
United States. I. Title.
TX360.U6F87 2016
394.1'20973—dc23
2015027903

∞ ™ The paper used in this publication meets the minimum requirements of
American National Standard for Information Sciences Permanence of Paper for
Printed Library Materials, ANSI/NISO Z39.48-1992.

Printed in the United States of America

CONTENTS

PREFACE

My love affair with food began when, as a nineteen-year-old, I was invited to a family meal at the home of an Italian friend. As the conversation, in all its twists and turns, always returned to the food and its quality, it was apparent that, for them, food was more than fuel or a pleasant diversion—it took on aspects of the sacred, something to be cherished in itself as a potent symbol of the good life. Since that memorable meal I have gradually become convinced that nothing else in life gives us so much ongoing pleasure as the food we love, so I was struck, when drinking deeply from the history of philosophy and teaching it for many years, by the fact that great thinkers largely ignore food as something worthy of thoughtful attention. Perhaps it is a sign of my distinct lack of greatness that I decided to devote considerable attention to thinking about the culture of the table and its importance to a life well lived. The result is this book, which attempts to understand why this fascination with food has become so prominent in our culture. I am afraid, however, that a book about food written only for philosophers might prove to be unsavory or go to waste, and so I seek readers among the general public whose fascination with flavor takes a thoughtful turn.

Even prominent writers who take simple pleasure as their theme seem to forget their victuals. George Orwell writes:

> I think that by retaining one's childhood love of such things as trees, fishes, butterflies and—to return to my first instance—toads, one makes a peaceful and decent future a little more probable, and that by preaching the doctrine that nothing is to be admired except steel and

concrete, one merely makes it a little surer that human beings will have
no outlet for their surplus energy except in hatred and leader worship.

What? No shepherd's pie or bangers and mash among his fond memories? I would suggest that the pleasures of life are experienced most directly when seated at a table laden with the bounty of harvest and surrounded by friends. And so I write with gratitude toward all those with whom I've shared a table and especially those who cook with panache.

Join me for more on the philosophy of food and wine at *Edible Arts* (http://foodandwineaesthetics.com/).

INTRODUCTION

America Discovers Its Palate

The United States of the mid-1950s was an unlikely place to launch a revolution in taste. In my lower-middle-class New England family, a piece of well-done beef or meat loaf, accompanied by instant mashed potatoes topped with canned tomatoes, next to a mound of canned peas, was a Saturday-only treat. Hot dogs and beans were more common. During the week, TV dinners were enthusiastically welcomed as a symbol of modern sophistication. Our nod to "ethnic" food included spaghetti topped with jarred tomato sauce, meatballs, and cakey parmesan powder poured from a green, cardboard cylinder. An excursion into exotica was accomplished via cans of chop suey—hunks of chicken, peppers, mushrooms, celery, and "exotic" bean sprouts suspended in a soy-flavored, corn starch–thickened sauce—served over Uncle Ben's converted rice. Chopped iceberg lettuce and tomato wedges were a salad. If fruit appeared at all, it was suspended in Jell-O. Wonder Bread was indeed wonderful. The dining tables of my better-off friends differed only in the quality of the china.

Even in high-end restaurants that served so-called "Continental cuisine" canned or prepared foods were too often the norm. Dishes such as crab casserole (canned crab with canned cream of mushroom soup and canned fried onions), beef stroganoff (hunks of well-done meat and noodles swimming in cream), or chicken divan (often made with precooked chicken breasts and canned soup) were considered luxurious. To be fair, the better dining establishments in New York had higher standards, but even at the famed Le Pavillon it is rumored that in the late 1950s frozen food had become the norm.

In part, the poverty of mid-twentieth-century American cuisine was the product of the deprivations of the Great Depression and World War II. But Americans have long looked askance at culinary sophistication and been wary of elitism, especially when coming from foreign influences. As recently as 2004, good taste was widely perceived as an indicator that one lacked genuine American virtue. During the presidential primary election season that year, a conservative political ad attacked Democratic presidential hopeful Howard Dean as a "latte-drinking, sushi-eating, Volvo-driving" left-wing freak. But there is a long history of this sort of political insult. In 1840 supporters of presidential candidate William Henry Harrison smeared incumbent Martin Van Buren as a "monarchist" because he drank French champagne and hired a French chef.

Throughout our history, puritanical religious leaders inveighed against taking pleasure in food. The Presbyterian minister Sylvester Graham, inventor of the graham cracker, railed against almost all foods except his beloved wheat because he thought they encouraged the sin of masturbation.[1] And food professionals have traditionally been more interested in health concerns than enjoyment, although their prescriptions were often faddish and without scientific support. Dr. John Kellogg, the late nineteenth-century Seventh-day Adventist and inventor of corn flakes, put it bluntly: "The decline of a nation commences when gourmandizing begins"—this from a "scientist" who advocated that patients eat nothing but grapes and chew each bite of food one hundred times.

The inevitable march of science gradually taught Americans, most of whom needed little convincing, that food should not be a source of pleasure but instead a source of fuel and nutrition. Even an authority such as Fanny Farmer, for much of the twentieth century the doyen of American home cooking, couched her recommendations in the language of science and nutrition. Historian Harvey Levenstein sums up the attitude toward food in the United States that was encouraged by the burgeoning nutrition science industry: "that taste is not a true guide to what should be eaten; that one should not simply eat what one enjoys; that the important components of foods cannot be seen or tasted, but are discernible only in scientific laboratories."[2] Elaborate meals with an assortment of ingredients were not attractive to people who wanted quick recipes with nutritional content that could easily be calculated. Undoubtedly there have always been pockets of great cooking throughout U.S. history, especially in immigrant enclaves where the flavors of home gave sustenance, but the general ethos was indifference to the pleasures of food.

How times have changed! Today, celebrity chefs strut across the stage like rock stars, a whole TV network is devoted to explaining the intricacies of fermentation or how to butcher a hog, countless blogs recount last night's meal in excruciating detail, and competitions for culinary *capo* make the evening news. Specialty food shops do a booming business in imported cheese or exotic, locally grown produce. Some restaurants carefully note the origin of their ingredients, tend their own gardens, or send the chef off to forage for local plant life. Neighborhoods are populated with coffee roasters, bakeries with fresh bread, and artisan beer and wine producers, and an understanding of how to make cheese has replaced knowledge of the latest hot band from Sweden among the cognoscenti of culture. Some middle-class consumers pay high prices for organic milk and vegetables and every town large enough for a traffic light sports a farmer's market at least once a week. Although we cook only occasionally and often eat on the run, we devote considerable time and attention to consuming media devoted to cooking and eating. Why this sudden interest in food? Have we Americans (along with citizens of the United Kingdom) finally discovered that our palate is more than a gateway for nutrition, or will this trend join the discards of history alongside pet rocks and disco?

The aim of this book is to explain this revolution in taste and assess its significance. Although this revolution in taste has been noted in the press and discussed by social scientists, there has been little philosophical discussion of this phenomenon aside from an occasional blog post. Why should there be if it is just a fleeting cultural fad? But I think there is something for philosophers to chew on here. The reasons why, at this historical moment, food and beverages have acquired their status at the summit of cultural significance are broader and deeper than is generally acknowledged.

It is easy to dismiss this interest in food as the new plaything of the wealthy and bored. After growing tired of sinking money into houses and cars, perhaps those with means have turned their attention to the next frivolous, hedonistic pastime, a changing fashion that has no more significance than a new line of jeans or a scandalous Kardashian photo. After all, there have always been gourmands with an inordinate fascination with eating well. How is this fascination with food different?

Furthermore, the celebrity-making machinery, having made heroes and then villains of actors, musicians, and sports stars, are turning their attention to new shiny objects to separate devotees from their money in the chefs, winemakers, and brewmasters that grace their publications. New forms of media encourage this kind of superficial engagement. Everybody eats and reaps instantaneous satisfaction from it. In an age where trading "likes" creates a market in moral authority, publicizing one's judgment about a meal is the kind of easy "expertise" that demands no sacrifice or effort, a form of entertainment that fits perfectly with drone killings, windfall profits, and virtual "friends." After all, does it really matter whether we eat quality food or not as long as it is nutritious and affordable?

The short answer is that it does matter, although explaining why it matters will take up a good portion of this book. In brief, my argument will be that the food revolution is a legitimate attempt to replace meanings that are lost when the bureaucratic, digitized reality of the modern workplace colonizes all dimensions of life. As to the complaint that the food revolution is just a hedonistic diversion for a few well-situated status seekers, this perspective does not fit the facts very well. Although many fine dining restaurants are participating in this revolution, their sense of adventure and risk-taking far outstrips the staid, conservative, tradition-bound, white-tablecloth establishments that status shoppers seem to prefer. Unlike mere diversions, food is now the object of serious study in multiple academic disciplines and the people involved in growing, conceiving, and creating the products of this revolution in taste are serious about their art for its intrinsic value, not merely as a source of income, which in the food and beverage business is often limited. No doubt the food revolution is driven by the pursuit of pleasure, requires resources to participate, and includes its share of frivolity. What significant human achievement is not so burdened?

Furthermore, the food revolution is not restricted to the wealthy. Many so-called "foodies" are younger people living on limited budgets, or bloggers who receive no compensation for their labors, and some of the most significant developments in the world of food take place in neighborhood bistros, food trucks, and small, family-run farms and production facilities—a labor of love where profit is an occasional (and welcome) surprise. There are too many aspects of this food revolution that don't fit the profile of a cynical, late-capitalist boondoggle.

That said, the food revolution does not affect everyone equally; it is significant because of its rapid growth and the way it has captured our cultural energy more than its overall magnitude. One aspect of the food revolution is the increasing popularity of local, fresh foods that avoid the long supply chains of large supermarkets that compromise flavor. Coastal urban areas and major cities throughout the country are all in. Small, rural towns not so much. USDA studies indicate the number of farmer's markets in the United States increased from 1,755 to 8,144 between 1994 and 2013. According to agricultural markets researcher John Ikerd, there were 2,700 community-supported agriculture businesses (CSAs) in the United States in 2009, up from about 100 in 1990.[3] Yet, according to a 2010 U.S. government report, "most farms that sell directly to consumers are small farms with less than $50,000 in total farm sales, located in urban corridors of the Northeast and the West Coast."[4] Ikerd reported in 2010 that overall only about 10 percent of the food sold in the United States is from "natural, organic, or local" sources.[5]

Localism is not the only indicator of a food revolution. A 2010 National Public Radio story reported that "data from the U.S. Department of Agriculture show big gains in Americans' spice consumption since the 1970s, including 600 percent more chili pepper, 300 percent more cumin, and a whopping 1,600 percent more ginger."[6] The Specialty Food Association's 2014 report states that specialty food stores recorded the biggest sales increase, at 42.4 percent between 2011 and 2013, followed by natural food stores, at 33.8 percent, with the Pacific and mid-Atlantic regions showing the strongest demand.[7]

Obviously, there is something going on here. This revolution in taste doesn't appear to be a "flash-in-the-pan" or a media-driven fad, although there is plenty of room for growth with significant portions of the population only marginally affected. Like most revolutions, it is driven by a relatively small core of dedicated enthusiasts which makes the attention it receives all the more remarkable.

A SHORT HISTORY OF THE TASTE REVOLUTION

Talk of a food or taste revolution in the United States is in a sense misleading. It is more like a counterrevolution and has been gradually picking up steam over many years. The first significant change in food practices began to develop in the early twentieth century with the emergence of new transportation technologies and mass electrification. Prior to the twentieth century, all cooking was seasonal and farm-to-table. Produce could not be stored except in cellars during cold weather and transportation was too slow to move anything perishable more than a few miles. Much of the cooking was done by slaves or hired help. But with the emergence of motor cars and airplanes, the speed of transportation accelerated. The storage problem was solved by the introduction of canning technologies, refrigeration, and later frozen foods. By the mid-1950s it was possible to harvest any food, then can or freeze it, and ship it anyplace in the world. Consumers could now eat anything at any time and, to the average consumer, this freedom mattered more than the loss of flavor that was the inevitable result of the canning or freezing process.

Meanwhile, women were entering the workforce, especially during World War II when men were off fighting in Europe, and were motivated to snap up any labor-saving device they could afford to get food on the table. Flavor, never a priority for most Americans anyway, gave way to convenience so that by the 1950s, writes journalist Leslie Brenner,

> the American housewife had been thoroughly persuaded, by this point, that cooking was a drag; new convenience foods offered a no-muss, no-fuss solution. . . . The quality of vegetables and fruits that one could find in the now-ubiquitous supermarket was pitiable; farming had become so industrialized that concerns of shelf life and transport now overrode those of flavor and texture. Fruits and vegetables, which the consumer no longer thought of as products of the earth, but rather as perfect objects forming geometrical displays in the spotless supermarket, now had to look good.[8]

Ironically, however, during the 1950s the seeds of change were sown. Julia Child, the future progenitor of TV cooking shows was cooking her way through France. James Beard, having been anointed "Dean of American cookery," was using his cooking schools in New York and Oregon to promote a genuine interest in food, and Craig Claiborne was transforming the sleepy *New York Times* food section into an authoritative source of knowledge about all varieties of cuisine. Meanwhile, soldiers returning from Europe had acquired a taste for European cuisine, and prosperous Americans were traveling to foreign lands and being exposed to exotic foods. Moreover, while mainstream America only dabbled in various cuisines of the world, immigrant communities kept their ties to the old country alive by preserving some of their food traditions, albeit significantly transformed by American ingredients. The role of these immigrant enclaves would play a crucial role in America's food revolution.

Thus, by the 1960s, the ingredients were in place for some Americans to begin their exploration of flavor. Yet it would be wrong to call this activity a revolution. Much of the action was located in New York, while the rest of the country was gorging on fast food and canned vegetables. The upwardly mobile were intent on throwing better parties, especially when the boss was coming to dinner, and this required at least the appearance of a trendy approach toward food. But this interest in entertaining was a means to an end—the emphasis was on impressing the guests, not on flavor for its own sake. In mid-twentieth-century America, food was seen much as it had been throughout our history—something with only instrumental value.

It is, of course, debatable at what moment any revolution begins. What seems sudden is often the product of a long, slow evolution, and this taste revolution was no exception. Interest in eating better for its own sake was slowly growing and needed only a spark to set it off. And that spark, improbably, was ignited amid the countercultural ferment of Berkeley, California. In 1964, Alice Waters transferred from the staid, conventional campus of the University of California in Santa Barbara to the political maelstrom of UC Berkeley and immediately became attracted to the sense of community that had taken root among the campus radicals of the Free Speech Movement (FSM). A trip to France awakened her interest in food, especially when prepared from fresh ingredients, and upon her return she proceeded to feed her friends French cuisine–inspired meals. These meals did not quite fit the "proletarian diet" through which her friends signaled solidarity with the poor. But Waters would have none of this. "As Alice used to put it, 'Just because you're a revolutionary doesn't mean your idea of a good meal should be Chef Boyardee ravioli reheated in a dog dish,'" says Tom Luddy, another UC Berkeley grad and member

of the FSM circle, who ran the local art-movie theater, the Telegraph
Repertory Cinema. Waters reportedly argued, "It's not enough to liberate
yourself politically, to liberate yourself sexually—you have to liberate all
the senses." Eating together was a socially progressive act that was threatened by the TV dinner/frozen food culture of the United States.[9]

With a little help from some similarly inspired friends, Waters opened
her restaurant Chez Panisse in 1971—an amateurish operation but one
that resonated with a San Francisco clientele who had traveled to Europe
and understood the idea behind this reinvention of American cuisine. The
rest, as they say, is history. Waters and her friends were responsible for
promoting the principle of fresh, local, seasonal ingredients, the importance of organic food, and the prominence of the forager, as the person in
the restaurant who seeks out the best local ingredients. Chez Panisse was
not the first restaurant to take this approach, which of course was common in Europe, but it was the first restaurant to succeed in amplifying the
message to Americans.

Herein lurks our first puzzle: The New York food world and the hippies of the Bay Area were worlds apart. New York represented the establishment, upper-middle-class bourgeois interests, the jet set that could
afford to travel, track down expensive ingredients, and leisurely play at
the good life. Waters and her crew were nurtured in the crucible of the
counterculture where material wealth was considered crass, if not immo-
ral, and the establishment was the enemy standing in the way of justice,
healthy communities, and a less destructive stance toward the world.
What did these two worlds have in common that enabled them to join
together in putting food on the cultural map?

Part of the motivation of Waters and crew was clearly ethical and
political. But as the quotes from Waters above make clear, pleasure was
central to her worldview. All the save-the-world rhetoric notwithstanding,
the food had to be exceptionally good, a commitment shared with the
food establishment in New York. But that establishment also had more
than a commitment to pleasure to bring to the table. They were committed
to finding and consuming good food, and as almost all food writing
throughout history has emphasized, food is about community. It is about
bringing together and nourishing the people around you. Despite their
vastly different cultural assumptions, both the New York food establishment and the countercultural renegades shared this commitment to pleasure and community. This confluence of pleasure and community is at the

heart of the kind of value food has and will play an important role in what follows.

Even after the birth of Chez Panisse, we are still a long way from the emergence of a genuine food culture in the United States, and there were many actors from Wolfgang Puck to Michael Pollan who contributed mightily to its development. The story of the principle actors in this revolution has been told elsewhere, so I won't repeat it here. However, this story as it is typically told leaves out something very important. The figures who now loom so large as historical agents in getting us to enjoy good food were able to have an effect only because people were willing to buy what they were selling. While Alice Walker and Julia Child were plying their wares, ordinary people were finding new ways to think about food. It is not just the wealthy or the terminally hip who are involved. The food revolution also penetrates deeply into the middle class, with young people, often short on funds, showing an avid interest in food. Why? There are deep historical and social forces at work that extend far beyond the celebrities and media hounds that explain why the public has been so willing to jump on board despite our historically weak relationship with the pleasures of food. My aim in this book is to try to understand the conceptual framework that underlies these historical and social forces and to show the underlying logic that pushes this revolution forward. I want to explore the meanings that food has acquired that have enabled this transformation in how we eat.

Although the food revolution is often thought to be motivated by moral considerations such as a concern for how animals are treated, resource depletion, and environmental/sustainability issues, food is an area where morality and aesthetics merge so it is hard to pry them apart. It will be part of my argument that aesthetics and a change in the importance of the pursuit of pleasure are doing the heavy lifting; the power of aesthetics to generate social change will be a major theme. Thus, to understand this revolution we will have to explore not only the production and consumption patterns of Americans but also the role of pleasure in a good life, the changes in American culture that have made food seem important, and the way emotions influence food preferences, as well as concepts such as beauty and authenticity as they apply to food and beverages. But if the importance of aesthetics (specifically, the aesthetics of food as both an agent of social change and a source of meaning) is a principal theme, then we must think about how the aesthetics of food is institutionalized and propagated through society. Thus, we must address the question of whether food is an art form and whether food has the depth of meaning and expression that warrants the attention we now give it. To claim an activity as a serious form of art is to acknowledge that it is not mere entertainment but something worthy of serious study and a source of profound experience. I will argue it is so worthy.

It might seem a bit of hyperbole to say that food has taken on a significance often reserved for spiritual quests and religious devotion. I think this is not hyperbole at all. In fact, I will argue that the realm of taste occupies a sacred space in our lives. There are good reasons why we worship at the altar of barbecue and jambalaya. The taste revolution cannot be halted; it can only be savored.

I

WE LIVE FROM GOOD SOUP

The pursuit of flavor is one path to a good life, a truth recently discovered by Americans that demands a new account of the meaning of food and its consumption. Any discussion of food and its place in our lives must begin with the role of pleasure. Yet our attitude toward pleasure is ambivalent: "Love People, Not Pleasure," blares the *New York Times*; "There Is More to Life Than Being Happy," proclaims the *Atlantic Monthly*; "pursue pleasure only in moderation," say countless sages throughout history; "it's only transitory," according to the timeless; "it is inimical to spirituality," the bodiless would have us believe; "it will not lead to happiness," the ubiquitous self-help books tell us. We spend much time and many resources pursuing pleasure but then condemn it with a fervor usually reserved for death and taxes.

This skittishness about pleasure rests on some assumptions that we carry around with us even as we surf the dopamine deluge seeking a perfect wave. The United States was founded on Puritan religious principles that link moral virtue to self-denial and reject the pursuit of pleasure for its own sake. Any indulgence in pleasure could put the soul at risk, they thought. We've never quite given up on that belief, and throughout our history, despite the emergence of a consumer culture dedicated to scratching every possible itch, we continue to suspect that all this fun will lead to ruin.

This ambivalence toward pleasure is one reason the United States was so late in developing a culture of food. Thanks to the hippies and the Francophiles we now have a more balanced view of pleasure. As psychology and neuroscience are only now beginning to discover, all human activity depends on pleasure. If we are to survive and reproduce, we must be motivated to find food, water, and sex; pleasure is the reward for those efforts. But even more spiritually laden actions are motivated by pleasure. As David Linden, professor of neuroscience at Johns Hopkins School of Medicine writes:

> Most experiences in our lives that we find transcendent—whether illicit vices or socially sanctioned ritual and social practices as diverse as exercise, meditative prayer, or even charitable giving—activate an anatomically and biochemically defined pleasure circuit in the brain. Shopping, orgasm, learning, highly caloric foods, gambling, prayer, dancing 'til you drop, and playing on the Internet: They all evoke neural signals that converge on a small group of interconnected brain areas called the medial forebrain pleasure circuit. It is in these tiny clumps of neurons that human pleasure is felt. This intrinsic pleasure circuitry can also be co-opted by artificial activators like cocaine or nicotine or heroin or alcohol. Evolution has, in effect, hardwired us to catch a pleasure buzz from a wide variety of experiences from crack to cannabis, from meditation to masturbation, from Bordeaux to beef. [1]

The plausibility of this thesis depends on how we conceptualize pleasure. If we think of pleasure as a singular type of sensation passively experienced and distinct from the activities that cause it—an aftereffect of our activity—it may seem relatively unimportant when compared to the actions through which we accomplish important goals in life. But if we think of pleasure as the inherent quality of an activity that makes it rewarding and intensely interesting, then pleasure would not only accompany but also motivate almost everything we do. The pleasure I take in trying to understand a difficult passage in a text helps me look more intently and fruitfully at it, and helps me avoid distractions that lead me away from my goal. The pleasure we feel when absorbed in a task is not something added on to the absorption; rather, it constitutes the absorption by reinforcing it. Pleasure strengthens our activities and helps us aim at their successful completion. Thus, pleasure is not some optional pursuit that we ought to suspend if we have the willpower. Pleasure matters to us because it is fundamental to our motivational states—we are wired to care about it. We should not treat anything so central to our existence with the condescension typical of our puritanical intelligentsia. The pleasure deniers are not fully comfortable with being human.

Yet critics of pleasure as an ultimate good do make an important point. Pleasure is not identical to happiness. A person could be consumed by joyful ecstasies but not be happy because happiness, unlike pleasure, is a long-term disposition. Pleasure comes and goes. A person who experiences lots of pleasure but could not make overall sense of her or his life or see it as worthwhile would not be happy. Furthermore, for many activities, pleasure cannot be our goal. An athlete experiences pleasure at winning the game, but during the game she or he must focus on technique and strategy, not the pursuit of pleasure. One of the great joys in life is the experience of what psychologists call flow—the experience of being wholly absorbed in a task. But maintaining "flow" is dependent on being focused on the task, not on the pleasure, which can only support the focused attention if we are not aiming at it. Thus, a hedonistic approach to life in which the pursuit of pleasure is always the dominant aim is unlikely to produce the most pleasure. We care about many things other than pleasure, but when we satisfy those other desires, pleasure will be present as a reinforcement motivating us to continue to care about them. The experience of pleasure is not sufficient for happiness, but it is surely necessary, and a life in which pleasure is not a persistent presence is a crabbed and limited existence.

Food and drink, because they are necessities and a constant presence in our lives, are fundamental sources of pleasure that keep giving day after day—assuming we don't take them for granted. A life in which the pleasures of food are not central is missing a crucial dimension of a good life. As noted, we cannot always maximize the pursuit of a single type of pleasure at the expense of other things that matter. Limits of time, resources, and the competing goods of a well-rounded life prevent a single-minded pursuit of pleasure. But because food for most of us—barring poverty or disease—is an easily accessible source of pleasure, to care little for the pleasure it brings is a kind of moral failure with consequences not only for the self but also for others around us.

Yet any endorsement of pleasure comes with caveats and qualifications from the authorities—whether religious, intellectual, or parental. That is because pleasure can be dangerous when pursued without reason and self-control. Addictive pleasures damage us and everyone around us. But again, some of our assumptions about addictions are not compatible with emerging science. Addicts in fact cannot feel pleasure as readily as the non-addicted and require increasing levels of stimulation to find satisfaction. Addictions and compulsions are pathological and no model for the genuine pursuit of pleasure.[2] Thus, we need to make a distinction between pleasure that we get from thoughtless, compulsive consumption, and pleasure that is freely chosen. Pleasure freely chosen is actually a good guide to what is good for us and what should matter to us.

This emphasis on freely chosen pleasure is important not only for keeping us healthy but also because certain kinds of pleasures are deeply connected to our sense of control and independence. Some of the pleasures we experience come from the satisfaction of needs. When we are cold, warm air feels good. When we are hungry, even very ordinary food will taste good. But such enjoyment tends to be unfocused and passive. We don't have to bring our attention or knowledge to the table to enjoy substances that satisfy basic needs. We are hardwired to care about them and our response is compelled.

However, many pleasures are not a response to need or deprivation. I can be perfectly comfortable, yet pleased by the warmth of the sun as it breaks the clouds and comes streaming through the bay window. A light snack does away with hunger pangs; yet I am still seduced by the smell of garlic gently sizzling in olive oil. These pleasures are the lagniappe of life because they transcend need. We experience them as pleasures even though we aren't suffering from their deprivation. Thus, the enjoyment of food when chosen, rather than forced, turns eating into something more than acquiring nutrition or staving off hunger pangs. Pleasure rather than the satisfaction of needs is the point of the experience. Such freely chosen enjoyment presupposes an excess of time, attention, and usually some resources—it is a dimension of life that is not bound up with necessities, despite being part of everyday existence. It is a surplus, a form of grace, and thus has meaning that is not reducible to a function and serves no purpose other than the enjoyment.

For those who have learned that the experience of food is not reducible to a function or purpose, we live to eat—we do not eat to live. To find meaning in life in the first instance is to find meaning in good soup, if I might use soup as a stand-in for all the small, delicious pleasures of everyday life.[3] We live from good soup, not because soup is nutritious, but because the distinctive pleasure it brings is fundamental to a meaningful life. Enjoyment is not something for which we must develop a use. It is not an appendage tacked on to the satisfaction of needs; it is a consummation of our relationship with the world, a fundamental aspect of having interacted successfully with reality. The twentieth-century Lithuanian philosopher Emmanuel Levinas writes, "To enjoy without utility, in pure loss, gratuitously, without referring to anything else, in pure expenditure—this is human."[4] To be human is to live decadently, and food and beverage are the most accessible forms of living decadently. Eating has intrinsic value above and beyond any purpose it might serve. We transcend the realm of need through pleasure.[5]

This surplus desire for good food is deeply meaningful to human beings. Food has the power to anchor our identities and stands as a symbol of a good life. But, more important, food also symbolizes life itself, for food represents our constant sensory contact with the sensuous medium that supports life from moment to moment. In Adam Gopnik's fine book on the meaning of food, *The Table Comes First*, he opens by describing a condemned prisoner eating his last meal. Gopnik asks, "Why do we think of food at times like these?"[6] I'm not sure we quite get an answer. I would suggest that it has to do with food standing as a symbol for our most fundamental connection with reality—our total immersion in a field of sensuality that constitutes life itself.

THE FLAVORS OF HOME

Eating is situated within the complex of activities involved with making one's surroundings a home—humanizing raw nature, drawing it near, marking it as ours, and creating a boundary that marks inside from outside. The production and consumption of food has traditionally been the essential activity of the home and remains so in most homes despite our frenetic lifestyles. But in eating we not only modify raw materials but also consume them. Nature is transformed into my energy though the act of eating. The act of eating is an act of transubstantiation—I transform what is alien, what is outside myself, into my own substance. Thus, the satisfactions of eating are correlated with an act of brute force. Does the transmutation of edible nature into the self contribute to its enjoyment? Do we eat to express our exhilaration in possessing the world? No other activity short of murder enables us to possess the world so completely, and only this kind of fundamental meaning would explain the role food plays in anchoring our sense of identity, belonging, and hope. Eating enacts our dominion over nature and symbolizes that dominion as well. The grip that food has on us, its centrality as an anchor for our sense of belonging, rests on the symbolic meaning of this transubstantiation. We don't kill to live, but live to kill, since much of our dominion over nature is freely chosen and not a necessity. (This is true of vegetarians as well; plants, after all, are living organisms.) This, of course, is not to say that we get thrills from tromping on tulips. It is not the destruction we enjoy; it is the assimilation, the transubstantiation. [7]

All of this suggests that food is not a simple enjoyment. It rests on a chasm of deep meaning of which we are typically only implicitly aware. Our active connection to reality, the fundamental way in which we interact with the world via transforming nature, is a kind of possession that underlies the significance that things have for us. The home is the site of this transubstantiation providing a psychological anchor for our agency, and food stands as the symbolic enactment for all that happens therein.

Other animals digest food to get energy. But among all animals it is human beings who turn necessities into enjoyments freely chosen, who choose to live decadently, and turn our power over nature into a symbol for what we hold dear. Of course, there are many human characteristics that distinguish us from other animals. Rationality has long been a philosophical favorite; the capacity for self-reflection and the use of complex tools are additional candidates for what is distinctly human. The capacity to live decadently is one characteristic among many. We should not privilege this capacity over the others but only add it to the constellation that is a human being. If one looks at human history, it is hard to argue that the pursuit of pleasure is subordinate to our other pursuits; rather, it seems ascendant. The enjoyment of food is one of the most ubiquitous of those pleasures.

In the economy of meanings surrounding the act of eating, this dominion over nature entails a kind of independence. But to see this we need to say more about the home as the central location in which this dominion is enacted. To live is to be enveloped in a sensuous plenum, to be surrounded by matter that we sense and respond to without thought or intention. When that immersion in sensation is painful, life is dreadful; when it is neutral, life is a chore, boring. Only when that sensuous medium contains positive stimulation do we feel truly alive. A home is a particular kind of sensuous plenum. At home, we are surrounded by a plenitude of sensations in which familiarity is the most distinctive feature. Food is often, although not necessarily, the most perspicuous sensuous medium in the home because so much of our activity there is bound up with preparing and consuming food, and its aromas and flavors permeate our lived experience. Because the home is a place of relaxation (unless the housework is unfairly burdening some members and not others) we are in a position to fully engage with this sensuous dimension without the distractions or turmoil of industry. When I succeed in making a home it individuates me—I separate myself from the rest of reality and the threat of the world, with its dangers and obstacles, recedes.

When hungry, this separation from the world, which I accomplish through the satisfactions of the home, is compromised because I am then utterly dependent on the world for my survival. When eating purely for pleasure, however, that independence is preserved. When freed from the pressure of needs I can then use my time as I see fit. The saturation of the plenum, the condition in which I am surrounded by satisfying sensuous experiences, constitutes my complete independence. Safety, satiety, comfort, and familiarity are pleasurable experiences because they represent this independence. This experience of saturation is what we seek with celebrations focused on the home. In the United States, holidays like Thanksgiving and Christmas, whatever else they might mean, are focused on creating this saturated plenum in the home. This is why they are so attractive and we go to such trouble to create atmosphere. We are thus moved to decorate our lives or at least appreciate such decoration. It is born of a fundamental need to escape need—to provide meaning that is not just responding to a lack, an absence of satisfaction. Even people who are living in poverty and are constantly faced with the task of satisfying needs have provided this decoration. In many cultures, the most vibrant colors and flavors come from the street.

Good soup, as the symbol of the comforts of home, thus provides us with the feeling of the world receding. The enjoyment of being immersed in the sensuous plenum of the home teaches us that this experience of enjoyment has intrinsic value—it serves no other purpose and is not reducible to its usefulness. For this experience, the quality of the soup matters. But its goodness is the goodness of direct, unmediated pleasure that does not require fine discrimination or intellectualizing. Its goodness is not recognized through critical judgment. We are simply drawn to its quality and can sense it. Its goodness announces itself to us. This is the

very nature of comfort food. The quality of the food expresses our dominion, our control over nature, our ability to create surplus. These everyday
experiences are not yet art-like. They are often passive and less focused
than the appreciation of art requires and have limited meanings that are
continually repeated, unlike art that is searching for new meanings. We
might consider it a form of kitsch if we want to be dismissive. But these
experiences are aesthetic and, as I will argue later in the book, have a kind
of beauty appropriate to them, and under some circumstances can be
appropriately called art.

This independence that we seek through our home-life is of course an
illusion, only a temporary respite that cannot be sustained. The realm of
needs inevitably and persistently intrudes. We will soon be hungry again,
will have to find resources, and return to the distractions and turmoil of
industry. As thoroughly dependent beings, we never achieve actual independence; for most people throughout the majority of history, the illusion
of this independence could be sustained only in an occasional moment
and at the expense of women who supplied the labor. The cook who must
struggle with nature knows better than to assert her or his freedom from
nature, but the pleasures of the home have the power to foster this illusion
of "refuge" as a temporary respite from the world of needs. Though an
illusion, it is no less meaningful.

These ruminations on the home as a source of pleasure and independence suggest that while we may scour the universe for signs of intelli-
gence, probe the brain for the roots of cognition, and build city after city
packed with buildings that reach for the sky, it is the small pleasures of
life that matter most to us. The eighteenth-century French philosopher
Jean-Jacques Rousseau wrote that "taste is knowing the tissue of little
things that make up the agreeableness of life."[8] The "tissue of little
things" refers to the everyday moments of satisfaction that make up the
real substance of a life and give life its character. The subtle gestures of
romance, the quiet certainties of friendship, the musical cadence of con-
versations, or the moments of a caretaker's resolve mingle with the som-
ber moods of a dreary day, the pleasant feeling when someone smiles, the
hypnotic rhythm of waves crashing on the beach, or the gentle rustling of
trees. These "little things" support the meaningfulness of life from moment to moment regardless of the major events that come and go. The
great pleasures in life are fine, but it is the little things in life that sustain
our engagement with life most of the time. Take away your favorite

foods, and life is diminished. There is a reason why a condemned person's last request is for a meal. Such enjoyment is direct, unmediated, and available to everyone, barring disease. The pleasures of food take center stage among this tissue of little things because they bear the mark of our freedom from needs, the surplus of life that gives life its grace. It is this surplus pleasure disconnected from need that explains the crucial role food plays in our capacity for sociality.

WHY CIVILIZATION RESTS ON FLAVOR

Even when the home opens up to the world by offering its hospitality to others, food still represents the idea of a surplus pleasure. Our generosity reveals the degree to which we are independent of need. Because our sense of independence depends on enjoyment, the whole edifice of the home rests on our ability to reign in our most powerful destructive desires. The brute force of our dominion over nature cannot express itself in conflict at the table. The enjoyment of food requires we pay attention to our internal psychological states while maintaining contact with others, and thus we must tame those unruly impulses that cause conflict and interfere with our ability to properly distribute our attention. Taste is one among several civilizing strategies that make a human life possible and for that strategy to be successful, flavor must matter.

Food is part of nearly every aspect of social life. Both our biological families and the families we choose coalesce around food. We converse with friends over coffee, tea, beer, a snack, or a glass of wine. Going to lunch or dinner with friends is the dominant mode of socializing in modern life. For many families, much of their communication takes place around the kitchen table. We share our tables with friends and family at celebrations where food takes on the ritual meanings of shared values or shared history. Even at funerals, at least at the wake, food is often served.

The other sense modalities do not lend themselves so easily to social life. Although the visual field is available to others, we seldom think of visual experiences as paradigmatic ways of spending time with others. Viewing a sunset or a work of art in solitude can be wonderful, the solitude enhancing the experience. With modern technology, we listen to music through ear buds designed to lock out the rest of the world. Although listening to music is sometimes a social occasion, and being part of a community of listeners can be important to some people, only rarely is sociality essential to the experience. Touch is a shared social experience only in the most intimate of relationships. Taste, by contrast, is the sense modality that, as a matter of practice, is intimately tied to social life. Although we can and do eat alone, we only rarely contrive to do so, and few would consider it an enhancement.

The reason for this intimate connection between food and socializing is not hard to discern. Given the time involved in, and the necessity of gathering, preparing, and consuming food, no other activity plays such a prominent role in giving form to daily life. We divide up the day according to when and how we eat. Thus, only the most solitary lives avoid implicating others in food-related activity. But, more important, when we eat and drink, time slows; the rhythms of the workday must decelerate, making it an ideal time for socializing. (Europeans understand this well, whereas Americans tend to resent the loss of those precious moments of "productivity.")

Food and beverages are so intimately entwined with sociality that they are more than an instrument through which we pursue social relations—they have come to symbolize social relations. It is hard to think about the act of eating without visualizing a table with others present, and certain foods such as roasts, casseroles, and pies, which are designed to feed multitudes, are a symbol of that socializing aspect of food.

This social dimension of food is the focus of most food writing, both academic and popular. Sociologists and anthropologists often view culture through the lens of food production and consumption. In most academic research, food preferences are markers of identity defining us as American, Mexican, or Indian. They are signs of social status indicating our level of income, social connections, or cultural importance compared to others with less refined tastes. Food is a fashion statement that sends a message about how hip or traditional we are. It is a signal that one is committed to certain values such as health or environmentalism, a form of seduction, a public ritual, or vehicle for religious or ceremonial meanings. Thus, according to this research, when we eat, we are not merely enjoying the taste of food but doing something else that has more significance than mere enjoyment. Food is a symbol system through which social and political meanings are communicated and relationships are enacted.

In popular genres of food writing, the social dimension of food takes precedence as well. Although the characteristics of food hook the reader, where and with whom one is eating and what they say or do become the focus. Often the people who produce the food and their trials and joys take center stage, the pitfalls and challenges of finding and preparing food providing narrative thrust to a story that reveals a form of life. Popular food writing tends to slide into travel writing giving the reader a way to imagine the intrigue or romance of distant destinations. Thus, food is employed as a kind of stage setting for the unfolding of a human drama. It becomes a metaphor for ruminations about desire, adventure, memory, or romance. While M. F. K Fisher, Jeremy Steinman, or Ruth Reichl excel at describing how food tastes, they are all really writing about the social context in which food is produced and consumed.

The prominence of this social dimension in food writing might suggest that the flavor of food is taking a back seat. I suspect that most people view flavor as of secondary importance in social settings where food is served. Although our social gatherings coalesce around food, the meaning of these gatherings does not seem to depend on flavor. Flavor assists with the narrow purpose of filling the belly, and once that is accomplished it provides the backdrop for whatever social dynamics characterize the gathering, and these can be understood independently of the flavor of the food on offer, the appreciation of which is understood to be personal and subjective. According to this conventional wisdom, the ceremonies and rituals around food, the social events that supply food with its meaning, do not depend on the quality of sensations provided by the food. To focus excessively on flavor is to miss the larger significance of these social relations.

I think, however, that flavor plays a more crucial role in social relations than this conventional wisdom would suggest. Food writers, both academic and popular, focus on stories that are driven by the dynamics of the people involved. Flavor need not be the focus of the narrative but rather functions at a more fundamental level as a precondition for the narrative—it hides in plain site as something we assume without needing to mention. Yet, without flavor, the stories about food could not be told.

Whenever food is provided to anyone, two attitudes are necessary— trust on the part of the recipient of the food and generosity on the part of the provider. (Generosity is less a factor in commercial transactions, a point I discuss below.) Trust is required because we take food into our bodies. We cannot hold food at a distance as we might view visual objects from afar. Thus, our health and welfare depends on taking food only from reliable sources worthy of trust. Generosity is required because acquiring and preparing food involves substantial time, energy, attention, and money. Because of this commitment, anyone who provides food to others in a non-commercial context must be willing to give without expectation of getting something in return. The cook or host, although often providing food for herself as well as others, is providing beyond what she needs—she gives more than she gets. The relationship between guest and host is not symmetrical, except at potluck dinners.

Generosity and trust then are core elements of hospitality, which is defined as the activity of providing food and drink to people who are not regular members of our household. The reason why food and drink are intimately bound up with sociality is because sociality requires hospitality. Hospitality may be the most fundamental meaning that food has because every act of social eating takes place only against a background of hospitality. Stories about food, therefore, have a subtext of hospitality. It is seldom the focus of the story because it is presupposed unless the norms of hospitality are disrupted. [9]

What does hospitality have to do with flavor? Everything! Hospitality is not limited to food and drink. The good host is responsible for someone else's well-being in general, providing shelter if necessary, cheering up someone who is down in the dumps, or providing diversion to someone who is bored. But this requirement that the guest's well-being must be served means that flavor is essential. Hospitality cannot be achieved unless the guest is happy, and that means that whatever is served must be enjoyable—it must please the guest. Providing food that someone doesn't like or being indifferent to their tastes is a failure of hospitality.

That hospitality involves a commitment to a guest's well-being is obvious. But less obvious, though equally important, is the requirement that the food be enjoyable to the host as well. If we do not enjoy our own food, then giving it to someone else has little significance because we are not invested in it. The kind of giving involved in hospitality is not like giving spare change to a homeless person or donating money to support a cause. In the context of hospitality, food and drink are not given to confer a benefit on someone. If in lieu of refreshment you wrote your guest a check, she would rightfully be insulted, regardless of the benefit the money might confer. Hospitality is a giving of oneself, not only one's time, labor, or money but also one's passion, intensity, and sensibility. Hospitality is a genuine welcoming in which one's uniquely essential being is shared. The host gives something of herself, her own sustenance, out of genuine concern for her guests.

It is interesting that in restaurants, where the motive may not be generosity but profit, the trappings and rituals of hospitality must still be preserved if the experience is to be satisfying. This includes friendly greetings, a helpful waitstaff, and a responsive kitchen. (Today, it might mean a perky waitperson pretending to be your best friend ever.) In the very best restaurants that survive over the long run, the management maintains more than the trappings of generosity; they have a genuine concern that their guests enjoy their food—because their own passion and sensibility are invested in it. Thus, genuine hospitality cannot exist without enjoyment—mutual pleasure is its essence.

However, the role of pleasure in anchoring the meaning of food has an even larger significance. French essayist and gourmand Jean Anthelme Brillat-Savarin recognized long ago that our food practices are attempts to tame unruly desires and that civilization depends on our success at this endeavor. Adam Gopnik recently summarized Brillat-Savarin's writing as follows:

> For Brillat-Savarin, gastronomy is the great adventure of desire. Its subject is simple: the table is the place where a need becomes a want. Something we have to do—eat—becomes something we care to do becomes something we try to do with grace. Eating together is a civilizing act. We take urges, and tame them into tastes. [10]

The possibility of civilization depends on our ability to take our very powerful desires and submit them to a discipline that encourages socially acceptable patterns of expression. We don't eat like pigs at a trough because the resulting conflict and turmoil regarding something as essential as eating would threaten the foundations of society. Of course, one could argue that it is not a concern with taste that tames desires but the enforcement of manners and social sanctions for violating them that does the work. We learn to share, listen, take turns, and argue without offending at the table when we are young, where parents can punish violations of social norms. But sanctions and moral disapproval only go so far. The best way to control a desire is by replacing it with another desire and the desire to savor food in a secure environment with no conflict is a strong one. Once the rituals of the table are in place, diners are then free to consider the aesthetic dimension of food, which then feeds back on those rituals reinforcing the fact that dining has become a fundamentally aesthetic experience. Part of the reason we don't nab food off someone else's plate or grovel face down in the soup bowl is because that is not conducive to enjoying the finer aspects of what one is eating. Good manners are not merely ritualistic behaviors acknowledging respect for others. They also facilitate the enjoyment of food which is no trivial matter.

No doubt, our enjoyment of food is subjective in that we experience the pleasures of food via our own mind and senses. But this does not mean the experience of food is private and narrowly individualistic. Our enjoyment is heightened by our sense of it being shared, and our aesthetic experience of flavor gains intensity from the sense of sharing something meaningful together, of communicating silently—yet deeply—by communally engaging the potent meanings that food bears. Furthermore, good food is something that can be enjoyed across racial, political, and class lines. It can be appreciated despite other differences we may have and thus contributes to social peace. The enjoyment of food requires we direct some attention inward, that we pay attention to our internal psychological states while maintaining contact with others. Conflict and tension interferes with that inward-turning attention. Taste is thus one among several civilizing strategies that make a human life possible, and for that strategy to be successful, flavor must matter. Gourmandism is not just petty, selfish fussbudgetry but also an activity that strives for a certain kind of control over desires, one that exemplifies a modest, yet very real, commitment to civilization. This is the insight that writers like M. F. K. Fisher and James Beard shared with restaurateur Alice Waters—the bringing together of flavor and community that launched the taste revolution.

Thus, flavor does play a central role in the meanings that food has, although it operates below the surface anchoring common expectations that are noteworthy only in the breach. Food cannot play its role in our lives unless the norms of hospitality and civilization are upheld, and flavor is one reason we insist on those norms. There is therefore a good reason why taste is the sensory modality that is most closely associated with social value. It is essential to the hospitality that makes most social relations possible. Today food has become a kind of medicine, a source of adventure, and on cable TV a popular spectator sport. But these activities seem only remotely connected to its fundamental meaning as the pleasurable medium through which civilization is enacted.

As food has become fashionable it has become fashionable to dismiss people with an interest in food as light-minded and frivolous. As is apparent from even this cursory treatment of the meaning of food thus far, there is no basis for that judgment. Food is deeply meaningful and plays a central role in human sociality. This account in fact raises ethical questions about people who lack an interest in food. If food is so central to human flourishing, do we have an obligation to take an interest in it?

There are many ways to flourish as a human being and there are many sources of deep and abiding pleasure. None of us can care about everything that is worth caring for, if only for lack of time, resources, knowledge, and the vagaries of personal preference. Yet much depends on the reasons given for a lack of interest. If someone were to claim to have no interest in the arts because, in their judgment, art is of little value and a waste of time, they would be criticized for being coarse and narrow in their conception of human flourishing. Something similar could be said of someone who is indifferent to the pleasures of food, or whose food preferences are excessively narrow, barring disease, moral objections, or old age, of course.

This idea that you could be criticized for food preferences runs counter to the conventional wisdom about food. According to that conventional wisdom, each of us is an expert on what we like and picky eaters are not at fault for their fussy attitude. If I hate sushi, I haven't made a mistake or committed a crime. I can't help it; I like what I like. There is some genuine wisdom in this conventional wisdom. Thankfully, we don't all like the same foods. But there are aspects of this conventional wisdom that are mistaken. We are not infallible experts on what we like. Our tastes change constantly and in surprising, unpredictable ways. Remember hating asparagus as a kid or never liking sardines until having them grilled on the beach in Sicily? We often dislike something because our experience with it is limited or because its presentation was unflattering. If our food preferences are too narrow, we never discover what we like, and we are well on our way to a life of blandness and tedium unless we compensate in some other way. The world of flavor is large and diverse and promises a different experience each day. Life is just more interesting when you eat widely.

Such open-mindedness about food can help one develop open-mind-edness in other areas as well, and being open-minded is a good habit to develop. Being inflexible and dogmatic is not a good way to be. In partic-ular, being curious about flavor is a window into other cultures, and if our preferences are too narrow, we sacrifice this opportunity. In general, if your food preferences are too narrow, you will experience less pleasure in life, be less curious, and have less self-knowledge than you could have if your preferences were wider in scope. Furthermore, if your food prefer-ences are too narrow, you inconvenience others and risk being disrespect-ful and thankless since you cannot fully endorse a gift of good food when served something you don't like.

That flavor matters, as a source of meaning as well as an anchor of social life, has gradually come to be realized, however dimly or obscure-ly, by Americans over the past half century. In this chapter I have tried to provide an account of the meaning of food, the recognition of which would explain the prominence that it now has within culture. But why at this point in our history were Americans ready for the message, and why in the early decades of the twenty-first century has this concern for food and drink reached cultural ascendency? When the tissue of little things is torn, life goes badly. And in our world today it is being shredded. The next chapter bears witness to this debacle.

2

WHY FOOD? WHY NOW?

The taste revolution begins as a small, seemingly inconsequential shift in our private habits. Throughout the latter half of the twentieth century, as a result of increased prosperity, travel abroad, and the steady pull of the pursuit of pleasure, we found ourselves fascinated by food. But this small shift in private habits explodes in the early part of the twenty-first century. Food becomes a matter of great cultural significance. In this age of global spectacle—global environmental crisis, the rise of the machines, financial insecurity, and political violence—why should the humble act of consuming food attain such significance? I will make the case that our preoccupation with food is a reaction and antidote to the increasingly demanding, homogenized, utilitarian public world that we inhabit.

In chapter 1, I painted a rather idealized portrait of the importance of the home and the role of food in the economy of pleasures that make life worth living. The home and its pleasures are an expression of human freedom, a place of privacy and refuge where the demands of the outside world slip away and our own preferences take center stage. When we eat, we consume the residue from the outside world destroying the object in the process, its essence now belonging entirely to us. Through this expression of our dominance, we are satiated, immersed in a plenum of enjoyment that demonstrates that we are not wholly governed by needs. We can take time from the work of living and savor a useless moment. Thus, eating for pleasure with familiar others out of generosity represents our happy alienation from the utilitarian world outside.

For many of us today, this idealized portrait of the meaning of the home and the "tissue of little things" that animate its activities must seem like a cruel joke. The home as a refuge of privacy and independence has been ripped open, its contents strewn about the public stage, threatening our ability to perform even an illusory escape from dependency and the task of satisfying needs. We live in an increasingly administered, standardized public world in which efficiency, profit, and measurable success at a task are all that matter. The public world of work and politics has always discouraged the intimate, idiosyncratic, playful activities that might distract us from serving the aims of business. But in contemporary life, this public world has gradually, inexorably colonized the private world of the home. Instrumental reason is now the dominant mode of private reflection as well as public reason. There is no longer any escape from the competitive labor market and, with digital forms of communication ubiquitous, the needs of others, mostly strangers, are a constant intrusion in our lives. The requirement to be noticed, to be responsive, to be whatever someone wants us to be intensifies with every cell phone burp and Twitter blast.

Our lives are now thoroughly penetrated by the production paradigm—the idea that more is always better, growth must be constant, and the measure of individual worth is how efficiently we produce. One main feature of this production paradigm is the compression of time—the relentless acceleration of demands with the apparent shrinkage in the time allotted for meeting them. This time compression is one of the paradoxes of modern life. Labor-saving devices really have saved us time, and many of us, excepting those who must work multiple jobs to make ends meet, have more leisure time than ever before. But it doesn't feel like we have more time. In the workplace, time-saving technologies allow businesses to more effectively track employees' use of time, ramping up minute-to-minute stress. Whole industries can appear and disappear in half a decade, and employees can expect to keep jobs only a few years before moving on, compressing the amount of time available to learn a job and make your mark. Meanwhile, employees are expected to manage their own performance as if they were self-employed. Five o'clock is no longer the end of the workday; we work at home, in the car or on the bus, at the coffee shop, or in bed on Sunday morning while liking a post on Facebook. Each moment is an opportunity for advancement and every space becomes a workplace, producing the feeling that we must give our entire lives to our employers or clients.

Although our leisure time has increased, it doesn't feel like leisure. As the number of goods available to consume explodes, the struggle to choose what to buy or do always feels stressful because choosing one thing comes at the expense of something else. With so many ways to fill one's time, the feeling of not having enough time is overwhelming, nagged by the sense that we could always be doing something else. Human beings are the new hamsters frantically climbing a ladder that leads to more ladders on a spinning wheel that does little but boost someone else's bank account.

While time is being compressed by the frantic pace of modern life, our sense of space has expanded to the point where the concept of place is no longer salient. Most public spaces are now commercial spaces standardized to provide comfort zones and facilitate easy access and mobility by anyone who might enter—a Starbucks on every corner, with vast swathes of every city resembling an airport terminal. While democratic in appearance, in reality these spaces are designed to coordinate economic activity across nodes in the global commodity chain, obedient to the protocols of external control, with every public space given over to marketing the same products to consumers seduced by ahistorical, transregional brands created by the advertising industry. In the process, genuinely local places are stripped of uniqueness and particularity. Each location resembles every other location, and only the occasional extraordinary effort on the part of the locals preserves a genuine sense of place.

As the production paradigm steadily gobbles up these inefficient remainders of life, we lose touch with reality. As we frantically try to produce and consume more, we pay less attention to what we are producing or consuming. At work we perform our narrow, specialized tasks while having little connection to the final product and how it is used. Our social lives spread across the globe in superficial networks of "contacts" where we interact with brands instead of whole persons, absent the face-to-face contact that could encourage bonds of empathy and respect. Commodities magically appear in the supermarket neatly packaged with a price tag to tell us what it will cost to satisfy a desire. We don't notice or care where the items come from, how they are produced, who produced them, or why they cost what they do. We know little of what goes on behind the attractive storefront that shields us from the reality of the lives that produced the goods. By "loss of contact with the real," I mean our tendency to interact with facsimiles of real things in virtual worlds where the representation of something—its presentation in the media, in its packaging, its location in cyberspace—stands in for real objects or persons.[1] The idea that something besides production and consumption should occupy our attention—a sense of community, self-examination, the cultivation of our ability to think and imagine in ways that make our relationships rich and caring rather than manipulative and expedient— seems quaint and unproductive, a waste of time. In the process we lose touch with ourselves, our own subjectivity, internalizing the self-as-commodity theme and hiving off all aspects of our lives that might harm our "brand"—a homogenized, marketable self. Even our vaunted and precious capacity to choose is endangered, for we no longer choose based on a sensibility shaped by our unique experiences; instead, our sensibilities are constructed by the hucksters and evangels of global capitalism, informed by their surveys and data mining that shepherd our decisions. There is no longer any need for the authoritarian state to control its citizens; the soft power of seduction and enticement, engineered environments constructed by "choice architects," are more effective than attack dogs and fire hoses.

This is the context that makes the food revolution meaningful. In the face of these pressures people seek authenticity, local control, and a hands-on, face-to-face experience that reweaves the "tissue of little things" at a moment's notice—the food truck as vehicle of salvation. It is no accident that the Slow Food movement, locavorism, and an anticorporate undercurrent are among the dominant themes in contemporary food culture. But, more important, people seek to preserve areas in life where creative playfulness takes center stage. For a variety of reasons, food is the logical choice for this rebirth of private creativity. We seek to recapture a sense of agency though preoccupation with our own sense of taste, creativity harnessed for the benefit of the individual instead of our corporate masters and the last place on earth where subjectivity rules. The food revolution is fundamentally an aesthetic revolution driven by a felt need to reconnect with reality.

INSTRUMENTAL REASON VS. INTRINSIC VALUE

What has enabled the production paradigm to insinuate itself so easily and so completely into our lives? The answer to this question lies in our patterns of thought that make the demands of the production paradigm seem so natural and uncontroversial. These patterns of thought, generally referred to under the rubric "instrumental reason," have been endlessly discussed by philosophers and social scientists over the past 100 years. But the concept of instrumental reason continues to have explanatory power in understanding developments in contemporary society, and the food revolution is no exception.[2] Instrumental reason is so common and defensible we hardly are aware that it creates a trap for the unsuspecting bon vivant. Instrumental reason assesses the value of an activity or object based solely on whether it is an effective means of achieving a chosen end. Efficiency, the best cost-to-output ratio, is its standard of success. It is not concerned with evaluating the ends we seek as these are thought to be a matter of subjective preference. "Save time, save money, save resources, but get the most!" is its rallying cry. Obviously any society, any individual for that matter, must be concerned with efficiency. We cannot squander scarce resources if we expect to flourish. So this way of thinking has existed throughout history. But it has come to dominate every aspect of life only in modern, capitalist societies where the logic of the marketplace has become the measure of all things.

The logic of the marketplace is simple. Businesses decide to sell whatever commodities will maximize their profit, and they will, if they are rational, seek the most efficient means of realizing that profit by purchasing materials as cheaply as possible, employing new technology when it increases productivity, seeking lower wages to produce more at less cost, and marketing to increase demand for their products. Because investors demand a return on their investment that is greater than the return from alternative places to park their money, growth from quarter to quarter is essential. Failure to maximize profit or to grow more than your competitors begins a death spiral that puts a firm out of business if it doesn't reverse the trend. What you produce or the quality of the product does not matter as long as profit and growth meet expectations.

The problem lies not with the goal of efficiency or the pursuit of profit by themselves but in the fact that this mode of thinking has come to dominate all areas of human life.[3] The result is that much of modern life has become standardized in order to fit the requirements of industry, activities that supply individuals with deep meaning are stripped of value and transformed into commodities to be bought and sold like bars of soap, and, perhaps most important, our dearest possessions—time and subjectivity—are stolen from us and sold to the highest bidder.

I will explain what I mean by the "dominance of instrumental reason" by invoking its most ubiquitous manifestation. The fast-food industry has spread like a virus throughout the world, and almost every type of food is represented in these chain stores that appear in every city, town, freeway interchange, school, hospital, and airport. This model of food distribution aims to maximize profit by providing us with as much food as possible at minimal cost and effort for the consumer. In order to distribute this food efficiently, it must be predictable, generic, and homogeneous so as not to surprise or offend anyone. Although some fast-food chains are experimenting with catering to local tastes to a degree, the food must be, for the most part, the same regardless of whether one is in New York or Biloxi. To achieve such homogeneity, each aspect of the production process must be precisely calculable and controlled (the exact number of hamburgers from a side of beef, tortillas of exactly the same size to fit into a container, fries uniformly cut so the identical amount will fit into each bag, vegetables that can be shipped without loss)—packaging trumps quality. Such standardization requires a production process governed by numbers and it places value only on what can be precisely calculated. On the consumption side, consumers are encouraged to value quantity over quality, since a focus on quality would introduce subjective factors into the equation that cannot be controlled by the producer. Big Macs, Big Gulps, and supersized meals measure our degree of satisfaction in precisely countable units. In fact, uniformity and standardization are so important that uncontrollable factors in the production process must be eliminated, which inevitably means uncontrollable workers are replaced by machines when possible. The world of fast food—so efficient, profitable, ubiquitous, and necessary—is a place of poor nutrition, low quality, and stultifying sameness all made possible by low-paid, alienated labor. Of course, fast food exists for a reason. Since time compression is a problem in a society governed by instrumental reason, fast food is the solution—the architects of the production paradigm are only too happy to solve the problems they create for a price.

The prevalence of instrumental reason is not confined to the fast-food industry. It is evident in the emergence of supermarkets in the early twentieth century, which replaced neighborhood stores and introduced inferior foods such as the modern tomato, which tastes like cardboard but is disease resistant; uniform in size, shape, and color; and thick skinned to enable transportation. It is also evident in a much different way in the emergence of what Michael Pollan calls "nutritionism"—the notion, promoted by health advocates of all sorts, that food is nothing more than a collection of nutrients whose sole purpose is to supply nutrition to the body.[4] According to "nutritionism," we can gain all we need from food by amplifying the good nutrients and minimizing the bad, an approach on which the food industry has capitalized in marketing their processed food at the expense of our more healthy and flavorful food traditions.

The 1980s saw the birth of another example of instrumental reason—convenience foods such as chicken nuggets, mac'n'cheese, and "Lunchables," flavored, packaged, and advertised specifically for children to help busy parents cope with their children's picky eating habits. Nutritionally empty but popular and easy to prepare, it's an efficient way to get filling food on the table with no fuss or hassle. Yet children fed such a diet live in a culinary "comfort zone" and are never challenged by adult foods that might expand their enjoyment of food.

Environmental degradation and overuse of antibiotics in factory farms, the countless episodes of food contamination each year, the depletion of fish stocks caused by bottom-trawling—the list is endless, but all sanction the use of harmful practices because they are cost effective and save time. As Michael Pollan has tirelessly pointed out, waste, abuse, environmental harm, low wages, and poor nutrition are endemic throughout much of the food industry; they have traded quality for convenience and accessibility. Our modern forms of food consumption have evolved to advance a form of dehumanization as well. Convenience foods and restaurants allow us to eat what we want when we want it, but the ritual of cooking and eating together while sharing conversation is disappearing from our family life, a condition made possible by factors beyond the control of ordinary people.

I've used the food industry as an example to illustrate the patterns of thought characteristic of instrumental reason, but these patterns of production and consumption have spread through every area of commerce and have sucked in the worlds of entertainment, news, health, and education as well. In education, preparing students for passing standardized tests and measuring outcomes have replaced genuine teaching. In higher education, deep learning and the cultivation of culture have been supplanted by the shallow, utilitarian ethos of the vocational school where students are stuffed with facts and outfitted with only those skills needed to enter the labor force. In journalism, real investigative reporting has been replaced by entertainment designed to gain "eyeballs" in order to boost advertisement rates. In the health field, caregiving is reduced to how many patients can be seen in an hour and snap judgments based on tests replace dealing with the "whole patient" as an individual. There is no area of life that is unaffected. In all these cases, we see instrumental thinking at work, the kind of thinking we use when all that matters is that we calculate the cheapest way of achieving a goal and where the best cost/output ratio is the measure of success.

To be fair, many people in modern, advanced societies are able to resist the march of instrumental reason and escape the worst effects of it. It is not as if there are no spaces in contemporary society where genuine relationships and authentic subjectivity can take root. The situation is not exhaustively bleak. But the trends are unmistakable and relentless. This kind of instrumental thinking has a long history that is the product of good intentions and still has some positive effects. Enlightenment thinkers of the seventeenth and eighteenth centuries thought that by achieving greater efficiency, especially through the use of science and social science, we could free ourselves from the limitations of cruel nature and make ourselves less vulnerable to misery, disease, and early death. And of course it worked up to a point. We are much less vulnerable to some of the vicissitudes of nature than in the past thanks to the efficiencies brought about by instrumental reason. The resulting standardization and homogenization have made more uniform products and services available to more people and with much greater convenience because they are less dependent on time and place. Convenience and accessibility are important values that we can't ignore. Industrial food production has succeeded in producing enough food to feed the world, despite inequities in its distribution that cause persistent hunger in some places. Furthermore, low quality is not always necessary. Quality can be maintained for a price, and the products of many global brands are exceedingly reliable and of high quality if you're willing to pay. So what is the problem?

The problem is this kind of thinking has no limits. It never stops to reflect on what is sacrificed or to consider that not everything that has value can be reduced to a simple calculus of profit and loss. The one-sided dominance of efficiency thus leaves us with a world in which all of nature is nothing but an energy source for technology and industry and human beings are reduced to cogs in a machine.

It is not surprising that instrumental reason has come to dominate human affairs. For most of human history, the fundamental problem confronting human beings was finding sufficient food, shelter, and other material necessities. Thus, we have developed a fantastically efficient economic system along with an ethic that has enshrined work, productivity, and a love of material objects as the centerpiece of culture. Instrumental reason has served us well in terms of production and consumption. However, we now inhabit a much different world, a world in which overproduction rather than scarcity is a fundamental problem. Climate change is the leading edge of the cost of the production paradigm, but we are likely to see rising commodity prices, pollution, loss of biodiversity, unstable economies, declining standards of living as more and more jobs are sacrificed to the rise of the machines, and rising levels of conflict as nations and social factions fight over the scraps of our increasingly dehumanized world. We have reached a point in history where new ways of thinking must come to the surface because endless production has reached a limit. Our attitudes to food and its consumption will have to change as well because our food supply is deeply implicated in these limits and how we confront them.

But these may not be the most poignant consequences of instrumental reason's tendency to consume everything in its path. Efficiency has come to so dominate our way of life that the target is no longer just nature but human beings as well. The value of efficiency penetrates our self-understanding so that we measure, calculate, and control ourselves and others, but in the process we consume what is essentially human about us.[5] How long will it be before these systems of control evolve in ways that are beyond the control of all but a very few individuals needed to make executive decisions?

The dangers of instrumental reason when applied to persons are profound. When instrumental reason takes precedence, each person is replaceable and has value only to the extent that she or he maximizes the efficiency of the system. So we micromanage every part of our lives, bent on getting the most out of our possibilities, doing more and more without stopping to ask whether it produces anything of genuine value or whether the activity has value in itself independently of what it produces. The result for many is a life of constant work at intrinsically meaningless tasks along with economic uncertainty due the absence of job protections or loyalty toward employees, both of which are thought to be inefficient impediments to progress leftover from a bygone era. Even those who manage to avoid adverse economic outcomes nevertheless experience a sense of dehumanization—a sense that one's identity is being determined from the outside, as an isolated producer, detached from others, from reality, and from our true selves, available as a tool to be used for the generation of someone else's wealth.

With this jeremiad in hand, it's time to step back from the details of our contemporary situation to ask what all of this means and how it might be fixed. My main point here is that our relentless focus on efficiency and instrumental value encourages us to ignore the fact that some things in life have intrinsic value. They are valuable not because they serve some other purpose but because they have a kind of ultimate importance that must not be sacrificed. We need more places in our lives where noninstrumental value can dominate.

The question of what has intrinsic value has been much debated in the history of philosophy. Among the candidates are pleasure, happiness, health, persons, works of art, justice, truth—the sorts of things we think are priceless and cannot be traded in for something more worthy. Why is it so important to conceive of persons, activities, and ideals as intrinsically valuable aside from any purpose they might serve? Attitudes of hope and care, which give meaning and depth to life, depend on it. The quality of a human life depends on long-term commitments to persons and projects that are viewed as irreplaceable, as having a value that is stable and persistent, and that cannot be traded or substituted without loss. Only when we view something or someone as irreplaceable do we have the proper motivations to sustain those commitments. I cannot perform the activities required to maintain long-term commitments to family or friends if I view them as easily replaced by some new acquaintance who might more efficiently satisfy my needs. I cannot develop the skills and knowledge required to engage in complex activities if I'm concerned only with whether the activity produced a profit today or constitutes the most efficient use of my time. Instrumental value lacks stability because whether something has instrumental value or not depends on fluctuating desires, whether it is useful or not, or whether an alternative would be more efficient.

In fact for anything to have value at all there must be something with intrinsic value. When a child asks why she must eat her spinach, her mom might answer "because it makes you healthy." If the child were to then ask why being healthy is important, her mom might say because healthy people enjoy life more and live longer. Should the child then ask why a long and happy life is valuable, Mom is unlikely to have much to say. A long and happy life is valuable not because it leads to something else but because it has intrinsic value. The more our lives contain activities and experiences with intrinsic value, the more our lives are infused with meaning. When we become preoccupied with instrumental value—when we look at everything as a means to an end—we tend to lose sight of the ends, the goal of all this frenetic activity. The problem is not that efficiency is inherently irrational. Reasoning about efficiency is important, but it is only one value among others. However, we have allowed this form of reasoning to colonize all other forms of reasoning, leaving a fragmented, partial person in its place, easily manipulated by a predatory economic system based solely on profit. We need areas of life that are immune to the destructive effects of instrumental reason. Yet we lack those areas of safety. Human beings are exposed, with no home to turn to, and their subjectivity turned inside out.

This is the context in which our peculiar preoccupation with taste acquires meaning. The focus on food and beverages, on taste in general, is a form of resistance to this increasingly administered world governed by instrumental reason. My reasons for thinking this are primarily not based on statements made by foodies, nor am I claiming people involved in the world of food consistently and consciously formulate their interest in food as an opposing force, although I think this notion is implicit in their activities. My argument is that the meanings that food has acquired and the practices and interests that culinarians have adopted render food and beverages an oppositional force, a set of practices that resist accommodation to the production paradigm and cannot be explained by instrumental reason. Food has acquired these meanings as the result of people implicitly reacting negatively to the dominant tendencies of contemporary life and seeking an alternative that feels more authentic. A concern with taste is the natural domain from which such opposition can emerge, and thus people have to a degree unconsciously gravitated toward it and have adopted practices that allow respite from the dominance of instrumental reason.

FOOD AS A FORM OF RESISTANCE

The activities of acquiring, cooking, and eating food are not only everyday activities but also activities to which we must turn several times per day. Each day is in part organized around our need for constant nutrition and this need pervasively shapes our lives at home, in the workplace, or on the move. The fact that food also gives pleasure is an essential part of its normative structure; we contrive to make sure that while seeking nutrition and energy the food and beverages we consume meet our standards of goodness. The ways in which we give structure to the activities of producing and consuming food, including the kind of pleasure we seek in them and the moral considerations we bring to bear on these activities, shape family life, influence the kind of social relationships we maintain, explain the texture of community life, and even help to shape our personal identities if we take on board these activities as essential to the self.

The purpose of chapter 1 was to flesh out this normative structure expressed in some of our food practices, and my argument here relies on that analysis. As noted there, pleasure is an essential component in food's capacity to bring people together and serve a civilizing function. And pleasure has intrinsic value. By "intrinsic value," I mean the experience of pleasure has no motive aside from the experiencing of it. Some philosophers have argued that pleasure is the only thing that has intrinsic value. I doubt that is true; as noted above, many things have intrinsic value. However, pleasure is essential to the valuing of anything because without pleasure the very act of valuing is empty. Pleasure is best understood as the brain's reinforcement mechanism—a response to the satisfaction of a desire that reinforces our propensity to satisfy that desire again. Thus, whenever we care about something, we are motivated by the relevant desires that will be reinforced by the pleasure experienced when desires are satisfied. Even when our care requires difficult and unpleasant tasks such as taking care of a sick child, to the extent that such tasks succeed in satisfying desires they are experienced as rewarding—as on balance producing a positive hedonic tone which we sometimes experience as relief.

The pursuit of pleasure thus plays a central role in our pursuit of happiness. However we define happiness, there is none without states of mind that persistently include the experience of pleasure; without pleasure the satisfaction of desires will lack the reinforcement mechanisms that continually supply us with motives to act.

With regard to food, again assuming our nutritive and energy needs are satisfied, our concern is with pleasure both intellectual and sensory—we focus on how food tastes and what it means. But because this experience is so pervasive in everyday life, it is one of the primary sources of intrinsic value in everyone's life. To discount the pleasure of food as trivial is to severely limit one's prospects for happiness. Assuming one lives with food security, food is always available, within our control if we pay attention to it, and not subject to the contingencies of other sources of pleasure, situated as it is within a network of small pleasures, the "tissue of little things" on which rests the meaning of life.

The felt attractions of this noninstrumental dimension of food and its pervasiveness in our lives are the first step in the recognition of food as an antidote to instrumental reason. It is a kind of intrinsic value that when taken seriously provides a rewarding, edifying outlook on life that puts pleasure before production, geniality before greed, and care before commerce. Of course, it could be argued that the production paradigm depends also on its ability to produce pleasure. We are pleasure enthusiasts and this enthusiasm is well understood by the minions and evangels of corporations and their advertising departments. Why is food different?

The production paradigm's demand for perpetual growth is of a piece with the demand for more extreme forms of pleasure, more intensity, more speed, stronger sensations, the explosive pleasures that come with violence, competition, domination, and acquisitiveness. In the economy of bread and circuses, the circuses most often win. These pleasures are available as commodities, the payoff for our hard work, the reward for staying on the hamster wheel, especially the reward for competing well. None of them express care the way food does. Unlike these explosive, but episodic pleasures, the pleasures of food are tightly woven with the pleasures of conversation, romance, the subtle, gentle pleasures that make up the "tissue of little things." By learning to love these small pleasures perhaps we can unlearn the pleasures of violence and domination that seem so central to American life.

However, the argument that the food revolution is an antidote to the march of instrumental reason does not rest solely on the sensory pleasures of food. The food revolution has additional characteristics that distinguish it from the production paradigm and show the significance of food as an alternative.

THE SLOW FOOD MOVEMENT AND LOCAVORISM

Above, I noted that four salient characteristics of instrumental reason and the production paradigm are time compression, the disruption of a sense of local community and loss of contact with the real, the loss of subjectivity, and excessive homogeneity that strives to sweep away differences in the quest for standardization. It is no accident then that some aspects of the food revolution have evolved to restore a human sense of time, place, community, and particularity. We can best see how these factors are at play in the food revolution by looking at the influence of the Slow Food movement.

This movement was founded in 1986 by Carlo Petrini, who was reacting to the opening of a McDonald's in Rome. Petrini rebelled against fast-food culture by preaching not only reliance on local ingredients, sustainable agriculture, and fair trade but also a style of eating that celebrates food as a source of pleasure and community. Despite Italy's preoccupation with food traditions, even they have succumbed to the ravages of industrial food production, and fast food is pervasive there. Thus, the Slow Food movement focuses on education and outreach, helping people rediscover the joys of eating and the importance of caring about where their food comes from, who makes it, and how it's made.

The explosion of interest in food traditions and the consumption of locally produced foods promise to significantly alter how we eat. Sometimes called locavorism, the heritage movement, or farm-to-table cuisine, the Slow Food movement has transcended its roots in Italy and is now a global phenomenon. In the United States, locavorism is now mainstream thanks to chefs such as Alice Waters, the writings of Robert Pollan, and Michelle Obama's campaign to bring fresh ingredients and minimally processed food to school cafeterias.

Moral and political ideology in part explains the influence of this movement. The Italian Slow Food movement gained attention when it intervened in the debates about European Union food and safety legislation in the late 1980s. By attempting to standardize various aspects of the food industry, the newly emerging European regulatory agencies threatened the production of artisanal foods linked to particular localities and cultural traditions that were central to Italian life. The Slow Food movement capitalized on the need to respond to that threat and it rapidly expanded, opening offices throughout Europe and in New York City. In the European Union, it has become an influential lobbyist on agriculture and trade policy, and it has had much success in developing travel guides for tourists seeking unique cultural, food, and wine experiences. Thus, it has been a key factor in the growth of public interest in the politics of food.

In addition, opposition to industrial farming and the use of genetically modified organisms (GMOs) is growing, as is the interest in eating organic food. Of course, food politics is not a new phenomenon. A battle over the production of bread in Paris was the occasion of Marie Antoinette's unfortunate remark about eating cake, and increases in prices or taxes on food have provoked revolt in countless countries including colonial America. But in Europe in the twenty-first century, food politics is directed not at scarcity or justice but at identity. The Slow Food movement's prime concern is to protect the diverse, local traditions responsible for artisanal food production and encourage people to eat local ingredients. The threatened loss of specific tastes and the local cultures that produce them animate this movement. They deploy the aesthetic and symbolic content of food in a search for a more authentic lifestyle anchored in local traditions, which then becomes the idiom through which political mobilization occurs. Thus, the Slow Food movement understands the food artisan, not as a conservative standing in the way of progress but as someone charged with the preservation of local heritage.[6]

This politicization has repackaged indigenous foods as an exotic item for gourmet consumption rather than a source of calories for ordinary people. In many respects, this is not so much the rediscovery of tradition but the "commodification of nostalgia." Memory, the conscious search to revitalize the past, replaces the unconscious folkways and habits that make up food traditions. This idealized representation of the past is a way of imagining alternative social worlds and collective action. The consumption of haute cuisine, once a symbol of bourgeois elitism, is now the site of the reappraisal of individual, local, and national identities. But there is more to this movement than commercialized nostalgia. The aim is not just the recovery of the past but also the experience of it in a new register. Modern life, according to Carlo Petrini, the founder of the Slow Food movement, is characterized by the rapid compression of time and space that erases or makes impossible certain sensory experiences. We are simply too busy and too mobile to experience the pleasures that exist around us. The Slow Food movement advocates not only the recovery of a sense of place in rediscovering local cultural heritage but also moments of contemplation and stillness that enable us to bring sensory experiences to consciousness that life at breakneck speed passes over, and this is often echoed in the locavore/heritage movements in the United States. As the Slow Food Manifesto proclaims:

> In order to fight against the universal manner of the Fast Life we need to make a concerted effort to defend the pleasure of slowness. We are against those who confuse efficiency with speed. Our movement is in favour of sensual pleasure to be practiced and enjoyed slowly. Through Slow Food, which is against the homogenizing effects of fast foods, we are rediscovering the rich variety of tastes and smells of local cuisine. And it is here in developing an appreciation for these tastes that we will be able to rediscover the meaning of culture, which will grow through the international exchange of stories, knowledge and other projects. [7]

Memory is entangled with the senses and recovering taste memories helps us hold on to the past. As Petrini said in an interview, "Slowness is a metaphor for understanding and enjoyment, of being able to know who you are and what you taste."[8] Thus, the Slow Food movement demonstrates the power of food to shape identity and transform that identity into a political movement with political consequences.

I will have more to say about some of the contradictions and problems with the Slow Food movement and locavorism in the next chapter. But my point here is that this movement has confronted the production paradigm with norms that block the trends toward homogeneity, time compression, and loss of community.

THE DO-IT-YOURSELF ETHOS

Although appreciating food for the pure intrinsic pleasure of it is central to the food revolution, there is another sense in which culinarians are discovering intrinsic value—in the production of food. From preparing home-cooked meals from scratch to growing your own vegetables, butchering a hog, or making homemade beer or cheese, those involved in the culture of the table have begun to wrest the production of food away from corporations and make it part of everyday life again. This tendency directly confronts the loss of the real, our tendency to lead virtual lives.

In terms of the kind of intrinsic rewards we gain, there is a considerable difference between cooking a meal versus buying some prepared foods and heating them in the microwave. (Tending a garden versus buying cut flowers or playing a musical instrument versus listening to music would also illustrate the same point.) Microwaving a meal of prepared ingredients requires little attention from us. Such meals are designed to save time and effort and be more "efficient." But in that process of preparing the microwaved meal, we are largely passive. We are minimally involved by following directions and can be doing something else while the dinner cooks. The activity of "efficient" meal preparation itself has little meaning except as a means to an end. Thus, the prepackaged meal is a mere commodity, a device employed to serve a purpose and cooking a means to the end of getting the food on the table.

Activities such as cooking a prepackaged meal are part of what philosopher Albert Borgmann has called the "device paradigm," which he views as a characteristic way in which we engage with technology in the contemporary world.[9] Devices decrease effort by making a good more available—packaged foods that require no preparation are such a device. Or, to use Borgmann's example, think of how central heating has replaced the laborious activity of chopping wood, filling and cleaning the hearth, and sitting around it to keep warm. Devices make it easier to accomplish tasks, but this replacement of labor comes at a cost; it encourages consumption by taking away engagement. To heat the house, we just flip a switch and call the repair person if it doesn't work. We don't have to know anything about the device, and our interaction with it is minimal.

Of course, it is a good thing that we no longer have to chop wood to heat our homes, an inherently boring and difficult task, and microwaves and packaged foods make busy lives much easier to manage. But this pattern of disengagement in everyday life is not always benign. Activities transformed by devices are often shallow and monotonous, and they involve little challenge or depth. The "couch potato"—a person passively watching television without being actively engaged with the reality that surrounds him—is the standard example of how the device paradigm works in modern life. Technology can enrich our lives, but not if it takes away our engagement with reality.

By contrast, cooking a meal, like tending a garden or making music, involves personal effort and discipline. We have to focus our efforts over a long period of time before our labor can create anything worthwhile. But it is not the labor and the discipline that are in themselves important. What is important is that they invite us to adopt an attitude of attention and respectful engagement with the world in which we live; they open up worlds in which we are guided by things other than ourselves. Thus, Borgmann calls them "focal practices." Focal practices call for exertion, skill, self-transcendence, perseverance, patience, commitment, and attention, qualities that device-enhanced leisure devalues.

Chopping wood involves some of these qualities of engagement but it is not a genuine focal practice. Unlike chopping wood, genuine focal practices involve the whole person, a full range of human capacities, in an activity that is inherently meaningful and in which we strive for excellence. The reward for achieving excellence is of course pleasure. Few things in life are as pleasurable as doing something well, especially when it involves great skill. The practice of cooking is a perfect example. The culture of the table involves more than just heating food and consuming it. It is a place where family comes together and ideals are acted upon and reinforced. It is a dialogue with culinary traditions, an intimate communion between imagination, ideals, materials, ingredients, and methods. As Wendell Berry reminds us, "A significant part of the pleasure of eating is in one's accurate consciousness of the lives and the world from which food comes."[10]

The respectful engagement with one's environment characteristic of a focal practice is wide and deep. Focal practices integrate body and mind, the acting subject merges with the environment in sympathetic union, and means and ends lose their separation. The sharp distinction between means and ends collapses with focal practices because the productive activity itself carries meaning. The final product is only the surface of an ocean of meaning.

Of course, all of the arts are focal practices—both the practice of the artist and the practice of attentive observers require the respectful engagement with one's environment. Thus, works of art have intrinsic value because they embody the highest level of exertion, skill, imagination, and transcendence of which human beings are capable. The finished product—the work of art—is the expression of artistic practice and that is why we value it, not just for its pleasurable effects on us but also because of what it embodies. The act of preparing food is similarly an expression of skill, imagination, exertion, and transcendence. It engages the whole person, all five senses, emotions, and our social and rational capacities.

Part of the meaning this do-it-yourself ethos embodies is the importance of play. Western culture belittles play since it represents something very powerful to be controlled. Play is where freedom and the imagination join hands, not on the hamster wheel of consumption and recreation, but as an exploration of human capacities, a manifestation of the self in action. The fundamental motivation behind play is the experience it gives us. We might play a sport in order to improve our health, but that is not playful since it is undertaken for some purpose other than the intrinsic value of the experience. The fact that we get some health benefit is good, but it is a byproduct of the main motivation when we are motivated by the spirit of play. When we play we value the immersion in the experience, the tensions and uncertainties that have value independently of the ultimate end of the activity. The activity of play is thus an activity that resists assimilation to the production paradigm. In modern life we tend to colonize play, treat it as a means of getting children to pay attention in class or learn the spirit of cooperation. For adults it's a way of blowing off steam or a mechanism for team-building. But this is a misunderstanding of the intrinsic nature of play—it is about pleasure in our activity and experience pure and simple and needs no further justification.

When the preparation and consumption of food is engaged in as a focal practice, this spirit of play takes center stage. The food revolution at times seems to embody this spirit, especially in the work of the countless bloggers who devote hours to developing recipes with little expectation of reward. Playing with your food is no longer an impetuous form of childhood rebellion but a way of bringing focal practices to modern life.

In play, we are released from the relentless need to categorize according to accepted norms, released from the demands of efficiency, and of the need to be a resource for someone else's project. Play is virtuosity for its own sake, an interlude from practical life and an end in itself, a place where style and romance rule. The food revolution represents the playfulness of art imported into everyday life, where it compensates for the loss of freedom of privacy associated with the home.

FOOD AS ART

Time compression, loss of a sense of reality and community, loss of subjectivity—the food revolution directly confronts these ills of modern life with alternative norms. By taking pleasure in the aesthetic properties of food, while seeking authenticity, connections with real people, and with a do-it-yourself attitude, we as individuals begin to take back control over our lives. In the face of a global hegemon that threatens to disrupt core features of human existence, many people across a variety of cultures have chosen good taste as an antidote to the way the production paradigm disrupts ordinary life. They especially resist the influence of advertising by developing their own standards of taste, not merely as an aesthetics of consumption but also as an attempt to remake one's sensibility by resisting the demands of a consumer society. The problem with modern life is not that we have taken pleasure too seriously but that we have not taken pleasure seriously enough—especially pleasure in the tissue of little things.

As I will argue in more detail in subsequent chapters, an interest in food and beverages engages the imagination and is an expression of beauty that suffuses everyday life with an aura of mystery that is motivational. This point requires much more elaboration, which awaits the chapter on beauty, but the consequence of that analysis is that food is indeed "the new rock music," a modern art form that is at least potentially at the leading edge of social change. Based on this conception of its role in contemporary life, the preparation of food and its complements are matters of deep cultural significance best understood as an art form, for art in general is a form of adult play.

Yet there are serious questions that must be addressed about how successful this will be. There are deep tensions and contradictions that threaten the coherence of the food revolution and its status as an oppositional force to instrumental reason. There is a very real threat that instrumental reason and the production paradigm may find ways of co-opting and colonizing our search for authentic pleasure. And there are conceptual difficulties in seeing food as a form of art, difficulties to which I turn in subsequent chapters.

3

GATHERING THE TRIBES

Revolutionary Food and the People Who Create It

What do Warhol's *Brillo Boxes*, the Rolling Stones' "Brown Sugar," and an Italian grandmother's prize-winning lasagna have in common? They express cultural paradigms, ways of thinking and acting that encode and communicate a way of life, a sense of what is meaningful, admirable, and worth doing. Andy Warhol's commercial pop art displays the world in which the modern consumer lives—the relentless repetition of nearly identical products that had already begun, in the 1960s, to colonize American society. The Rolling Stones embody and transmit the world of bohemian revolt, the rejection of puritan morality and middle-class culture that motivated the counterculture of the 1960s and early 1970s. These works of art do not merely represent an idea; they create and foreclose possibilities for thinking and acting.

The philosopher Martin Heidegger used the idea of "world" to refer to the way works of art create a comprehensive framework of looking, feeling, and acting. The "world" of a Warhol painting or song by the Stones gathers together the practices of a group of people and demonstrates how these practices make sense as guidelines or possibility matrices for action, highlighting their central features and their "look" and "feel." They provide exemplars of a cultural style in terms of which we act, build habits, conceive of goals, and relate to each other. The "world" of a Stones song is a place where exploitation and exploration are inextricably linked in a quest to free oneself from the constraints of social convention. Their petulant, aggressive vulgarity, although an antidote to conformity, was performed with an irony that made the quest for authentic rebellion seem unachievable. Similarly, the "world" of a Warhol painting is stocked with depthless, superficial images that appear to celebrate consumer culture but lose their meaning through repetition—a mixture of cool irony and unbridled enthusiasm that prescribes a mode of survival in a world colonized by "product." The 1960s didn't invent irony, but they made it popular and accessible, and artists such as Warhol and the Stones provided the ground rules for participation in culture while remaining an outsider.

The traditional Italian meal, when it is most perfectly enacted, performs a similar function by providing stylistic ground rules, albeit with less irony. The Italian meal is not merely a cultural symbol; it produces, transmits, and reproduces central features of Italian culture and identity. The dominant trait of Italian cooking is its simplicity. Italian cooking does not involve a lot of complex modification of basic ingredients. Although sauces are important, most are uncomplicated combinations of a few ingredients that do not involve the endless straining and refining of stock one finds in French cuisine. Italian cuisine tends to eschew tricky procedures to modify texture or to build layers of flavor, in contrast to French dishes such as chicken galantine or cassoulet. Because of this tendency toward simplicity, a foundation of high-quality, fresh ingredients in remarkable variety is essential to Italian cooking. The doyen of Italian cooking, Marcella Hazan, described her taste as "free of affectation, taste that was clear, bold, and simple, taste that wanted only to be good."[1]

The most recognizable feature of Italian cuisine is the lengthy, multicourse meal—an event that may traverse an entire day. Italian meals begin with *antipasto*—hot or cold appetizers—followed by the *primo*, which consists of a small portion of pasta, gnocchi, soup, polenta, or risotto. After a suitable delay, the *secondo*, the main course, arrives consisting of fish or meat, accompanied by a *contorno* or side dish, usually a salad. Then, after several bottles of wine and much conversation, a dish of cheese and fruit appears and later in the evening a small dessert, perhaps accompanied by espresso, and capped by *digestivos*, Italian liquors such as limoncello or amaretto.

An Italian meal is a "world" that avoids fussy complexity, where ripeness, skilled butchery, and distinct flavors are more important than artifice and calculation, where a humble root can be as praiseworthy as an expensive cut of meat. It is a place where hours of relaxed, informal savoring effortlessly achieved is a statement about how life ought to be. Carefully wrought elegance, durable as opposed to trendy, classic, and genuine but appearing artless, achievable only through a tradition of allure and refinement passed down through generations. That is Italian style as a way of life, or at least that is the romantic vision encouraged by the tourist industry. Of course, in the realm of art, imagination matters. But the worry is that the romantic image of bucolic, leisurely meals, exquisitely prepared and presented, is kitsch—an easily accessible form of pleasure, sentimental and calculated for popular appeal, that demands no commitment, understanding, or challenge, the savory equivalent of a Thomas Kinkade or Celine Dion. Thus, we must try to grasp the kernel of serious purpose that lies behind the culture of the table.

What does it mean for food and wine to "express" this tradition of the Italian meal, which I am here using as a stand-in for many cultures of the table? What exactly is being expressed? The answer is style that reveals a sensibility. Just as Mick Jagger's swaggering, clownish naughtiness and Warhol's cool, ironic fascination with product and celebrity insinuate a particular approach to life, Italian foodways signify a sensibility that embodies attitudes, beliefs, and expectations about taste, family, time, and life as well. The importance of everyday pleasure is the persistent theme, for, above all else, Italian food puts an accessible, sustainable pleasure on the table and commands attention to its enjoyment. The flavors and textures of the Italian meal, the choices of ingredients and methods, the pace of the meal and the way it is served teach us that pleasure needs no other purpose or justification. It is not an instrument for some other aim, not a tool for achieving a result, except to bring the intrinsic value of the pleasures of the table clearly into focus, with the meaning of life encoded and communicated in flavors and textures.

Thus, Italian cooks (and not only the Italians) share, with Warhol and the Stones, the practice of artistic expression. Artists take culturally significant ideas and put them on display by glamorizing what for most of us is hidden in everydayness. When we are caught up in the routines of everyday life we tend to focus on the ordinary, the same, and the useful— dependability matters most. Our everyday world is like water to a fish— we are so surrounded by it that it goes unrecognized, and fundamental values that give direction to life become invisible. The job of the artist is to focus on what is suppressed, taken for granted, or lurking in the background of everyday life and bring out something alluring in it that will make us take notice.[2] Art puts fundamental values on display and invests them with majesty and grandeur—even when they also achieve ironic detachment as in the case of Warhol or the Stones.

Creative cooks and chefs express fundamental values through their art as well, even when collaborating with the tourist industry. Cooking is an everyday affair with its routines, habits, and familiarities born of the constant need to stay nourished. The creative chef takes these routines and habits and presents them in an arresting way that renews food traditions. They present the style of their tradition over and over again, but they do so as if we were experiencing it for the first time. In bringing this "world" to our attention, they foster meaning and meld a culture just as they integrate a well-balanced sauce.[3] Thus, the artistry of food not only represents a tradition and takes a tradition as its subject matter but also helps to sustain and renew traditions by focusing attention on the quality of a way of life, the shared style of a people, and brings it to awareness by glamorizing or ennobling it, thus producing a collective understanding that motivates further action.[4] This is why food appreciation so easily slips from mouth taste to moral taste. People get up in arms about food and go to great lengths to maintain their connection to home cooking, because it expresses a particular way of life and has a moral resonance that goes beyond mere savoring.

It is ironic that when art is considered as a means of expressing and integrating cultural affiliations, food and music are much more successful than the visual arts, which some take to be the paradigmatic art form. Although Warhol's paintings articulated at least some dimensions of a way of life, they were never popular enough to anchor a culture as did the traditional Italian meal or rock music in the 1960s. There were no pilgrims on a hajj to the Museum of Contemporary Art paying homage to *Brillo Boxes*. For art to play this role, it must be popular and pervasive; yet I can't think of works of visual art that have had such an impact. Food and music seem better able to gather the tribes.

FOOD AND THE AVANT-GARDE

Perhaps the best contemporary example of the culinary arts as cultural vortex is the Slow Food movement in Italy, described in some detail in chapter 2. The Slow Food movement encourages patient, artful savoring and the use of fresh, local ingredients typical of the traditional Italian meal. Yet, despite their ability to enchant and call attention to a tradition, the Slow Food movement and the revival of Mama's prize-winning lasagna have their limitations as an art form. They both seek recovery of an idealized past, and thus any innovations must not violate the threads of memory and attachment that hold their community together. The Stones, by contrast, although reaching back to the blues for inspiration, were sending rock culture off in new directions, a tribe of the future trying to slough off the past. Thus, as a paradigm of how food can be expressive, the Italian meal stirs only those emotions that rely on continuity with the past for their power and thus run the risk of being merely kitsch. How should a creative chef approach artistic representation in a tradition so intensely devoted to rustic simplicity? No mere repetition of classic dishes can count as an art, at least as art is understood among the moderns. We expect innovation and challenge from works of art, not mere imitation. But how can one be innovative while maintaining a connection to tradition? If food and wine are to be considered works of art, they must be agents of change. But chefs waving spatulas and shouting *viva la rivoluzione* may live only as parody. It is a pity that John Cleese did not think of it.

It hasn't always been so, but in the modern world we expect art to be revolutionary, to disrupt how we think and feel, thereby transforming the viewer or listener. Such expectations, perhaps, began when French artists threw down the gauntlet to the art establishment in 1863 Paris by creating the "Salon des Refusés," a maverick exhibition of works refused admission to the official Paris Salon. These works, scorned by the establishment, were the first stirrings of impressionism, which took liberties with color and line in order to focus attention on the play of light and a new way of viewing nature. But the impulse for artists to be in the vanguard of cultural change was present even in the Italian Renaissance when figures from the Bible were represented in a natural, everyday manner, in sharp contrast to the stylized and formal Byzantine and Gothic representations.

The first use of the term *avant-garde* to apply to visual art is reputed to be from the French political writer Henri de Saint-Simon in 1825. He declared that artists were in the forefront, the avant-garde, of social progress, ahead of even scientists and industrialists. He argued that artists are a social elite well equipped to sense the pulse of the times and reveal it to the public. Their job is to challenge the status quo and be ahead of their time. This idea gathered steam and propelled the modernist movements in early twentieth-century art, literature, and music. Today, we have thankfully dropped the idea that there is something uniquely prescient or prophetic about artists. Their crystal ball seems as murky as anyone's. Furthermore, we have come to suspect that marking a difference between the progressive and the incomprehensible is never straightforward. Nevertheless, we expect artists to not only strive for novelty and originality but also challenge, surprise, disturb, and sometimes shock us. Art is the area of culture where almost anything goes, convention can be flouted, negative emotions played with, and boundaries crossed. It is where imagination is allowed free reign, and where, sometimes, new forms of life find their first tentative formulation. If we are to discover resistance to the dominance of instrumental reason, we will likely find it in the arts.

The artist as cultural provocateur is often more myth than substance. The art world encourages a lot of aimless, ineffectual fooling around. Any institution charged with creating works that are both new and profound is bound to fail most of the time. But art sometimes achieves something genuinely revolutionary when it taps into forces already present in culture percolating below the surface for which the ground has already been prepared. Among the best recent examples of revolutionary art work are the more substantive examples of rock music that flourished in the 1960s and nourished that decade's cultural revolutions. Rock music did not spontaneously arise from nothing. It successfully exploited traditions of romantic individualism, the Beat movement, and the cult of the outlaw, along with idioms from African American and folk traditions to create its stew of characters and sounds that animated the be-ins, sit-ins, love-ins, and drop-outs that profoundly reshaped American society, for better and worse. In other words, rock music latched on to undercurrents, marginal practices already existing in society, and brought them to the surface, reinterpreting them and helping to make them central.

This residual commitment to innovation from the avant-garde movement poses an obstacle to food or beverages as forms of art. We seldom like to be challenged or shocked by what we eat. Our tastes are inherently conservative. The past inevitably shapes our palates, and expectation plays an important role in what we taste and enjoy. Furthermore, because we take food into our bodies, we have powerful biological reactions to unfamiliar foods that might be dangerous. Given these limitations, can food play the role of cultural provocateur, and is that compatible with the community-gathering function of food?

For a time during the summer of 2012, the blogosphere was rife with the claim that food was the new rock, coinciding with Googamooga, a desultory, overhyped food and music event held in Brooklyn. Despite its limitations, it did raise the question of whether our society's recently acquired, intense focus on food has the potential to significantly shape culture. Over the past decade, two important developments in the food scene in the United States have the potential for significant social change. One is the birth of modernist cuisine. The second is the emergence of locavorism and farm-to-table dining inspired by the Slow Food movement. Do these represent a kind of avant-garde of the food world, disrupting conventions and enabling us to imagine new ways of living?

"Molecular gastronomy" is the rather barbarous term originally used to describe a form of cooking that employs materials and techniques long employed in the laboratories of the food industry to create new dishes and taste sensations. It is now more often and more precisely called "modernist cuisine," or "avant-garde cuisine," because it promises to revolutionize traditional cooking and transform the emotional and sensory dimensions of eating. The use of the terms *modernist* or *avant-garde* to describe this form of cooking is no accident. The chefs at the cutting edge of this movement have aspirations not unlike those of the original avant-garde artists. They consider traditional techniques obsolete and too limiting; cooking can move forward creatively only if scientifically grounded techniques replace the old ways. Thus, modernist cuisine not only explores the science of cooking but also uses that knowledge to introduce nontraditional aromas, flavor profiles, textures, and appearances to provide diners with unique experiences. The result is dishes such as strip steak with beetroot froth, liquid olives, caviar-capped white chocolate, or eggs Benedict with deep-fried hollandaise sauce. The use of fuming flasks of liquid nitrogen, syringes, water baths, PH meters, and ingredients such as

carrageenan, maltodextrin, and xanthan gum suggests an unnatural, syn-
thetic, dehumanizing approach to food. But most of the ingredients are of
biological origin, and modernist chefs deploy this equipment in routine
activities such as maintaining the temperature of the cooking water, cool-
ing food quickly at extremely low temperatures, and extracting flavor
from food—tasks that traditional cooks have always performed, albeit
less comprehensively and efficiently. These ingredients and techniques
have been used in the food industry for decades; modernist chefs are
simply bringing them into the restaurant.

The term *molecular* is in fact misleading. All cooking modifies mole-
cules. There is nothing new about that. Modernist chefs seek a deeper
understanding of how we do so and better ways of doing it using the tools
of chemistry and physics to gain precise control over temperature, humid-
ity, pressure, and texture. Thus, they employ practices already present in
culture but transform them to achieve new ends. Thus far, the movement
has influenced some chefs at high-end dining establishments, and if the
discussion on the Internet is an indicator, many amateur chefs are busy
pouring over tomes such as *Modernist Cuisine at Home* by the guru of
this new movement, Nathan Myhrvold. At the very least, they have encouraged greater interest in the science of cooking, which has exploded in
recent years.

All this interest in new techniques will gradually influence how we
cook; some of these techniques are filtering down to cooking magazines,
as is the general interest in the chemistry of food. But will it remain more
than an interesting sidebar to the persistence of more traditional forms of
cooking? It is probably too early to say, but restaurants committed to
modernist cuisine flourish only in major cities and interest in it seems to
be waning as diners look for the next new trend. The modernist's view
that traditional techniques and ingredients are obsolete may be a minority
viewpoint.

The explosion of interest in food traditions and the consumption of
locally produced foods is the second contemporary trend that promises to
dramatically alter how we eat. Variously called locavorism, the heritage
movement, or farm-to-table cuisine, it was inspired and advanced by the
Slow Food movement but has roots in traditional, everyday French cuisine and the American and British culinarians such as Alice Waters and
Elizabeth David, who promoted it in the English-speaking world.[5]

With the emergence of this interest in local, community-based food and knowledge of the origins of one's food, the pursuit of pleasure has become an ethical and political duty for many people. Yet it is ironic that if we took the advice of the Slow Food movement's founder Carlo Petrini to eat locally, we in the rest of the world would stop buying the imported Italian foods that Petrini's organization has worked so hard to promote. Many of the producers who benefit from Italy's regime of legal protections for foods produced in their traditional regions survive by selling their products abroad to those of us who prefer to eat globally. The slow-down-and-taste-the-tomatoes ethic advocated by Petrini and locavores in the United States may be an antidote to the hectic, heedless activity of modern life, but it is an antidote so at odds with globalizing trends that it seems anything but avant-garde. Once the globalization genie had been released from confinement, exhortations to "eat local" have had to compete with the cacophony of alternative exhortations that set our gaze far over the horizon. This is in part because the "fast life" in our highly mobile society is not bereft of sensory experience. The "fast life" may make us numb to locally available experiences, but it makes possible new experiences every bit as fascinating and worthy of contemplation. Arguably, it has been the explosion of new flavor sensations from all over the world that has provoked this new interest in eating well and eating thoughtfully on which the Slow Food/locavore/heritage movement has capitalized. We might make progress by symbolically rediscovering the past, as these movements suggest, but such progress will not come from artificially limiting experience by commanding a rigid adherence to localism.

Problems with the Slow Food movement are even more evident when we consider the American experience, which is quite different from that of Italy. In the United States, virtually every town with a crossroads and a gas station now has a farmer's market. Restaurants promote their local vegetables and meat. Food writers glowingly write of delicate lamb raised on local farms, sweet shrimp hauled from local waters, or a crisp carrot plucked from local soils. We continue to embrace a natural farm-to-table ethos that is spreading beyond fine-dining restaurants and into cafés and neighborhood lunch spots. More and more menus are including seasonal produce and locally caught, sustainable seafood and boasting of the small farms and purveyors they utilize. Even the restaurant roof garden has sprouted in unlikely urban places. But, unlike Italy, the United States has never been concerned with legally protecting the origins of particular foods (or wines). And having invented the modern form of a "mobile society," the United States lacks the fascination with place that is so central to Italy. Rather, in America the prescription to "eat local" is driven by health concerns, mistrust of the industrial food system, concerns about global warming, and the search for quality.

As in Italy, eating locally in the United States is nothing new. Almost all eating was local until the mid-twentieth century. But new trade policies, industrial farming techniques, and modern transportation infrastructure now allow us to eat strawberries in January, fresh peas in August, and oysters year-round. Unlike most people in the developing world, eating locally for U.S. citizens is a matter of choice, a response to industrial food widely perceived as lacking in flavor and nutrients. Although environmentalism and health are part of the picture in Italy, they occupy center stage in the United States. Some environmentalists claim local eating reduces fuel consumption and the atmospheric carbon-loading that produces climate change, and health gurus extol the virtues of fresh ingredients and minimally processed foods.

However, the evidence that eating locally limits environmental damage is far from compelling. The mode of transportation used to get products to market is much more important than distance in determining carbon footprint. Given the size and efficiency of modern ships, it is often more efficient to move produce across the ocean than to truck it down the freeway.[6] The production of some foods, especially beef, is carbon intensive regardless of their origin. Furthermore, eating locally is simply not an option for much of the world. Billions of people live in areas where they cannot readily produce all the food they need, especially in the winter months, and the shipping industry has played a central role in making food available to them. For much of the world, "food" does not refer to high-quality fruits and vegetables, specialty meats, and artisanal cheese, but refers instead to large quantities of corn, rice, and soybeans shipped from industrial farms in the developed world. Many undeveloped countries rely on food exports to developed countries to maintain their living standards. If markets in the United States or Europe were to close because of a message to "eat locally," millions of poor farmers and agricultural workers in developing countries would lose their livelihood. In short, locavorism cannot feed the world or save the planet.

The health claims of locavorism are on more solid ground. Food that spends days traveling in a truck or ship will lose nutritional quality, and the processing used to enhance flavor in packaged foods is an unhealthy amalgam of salt, sugar, chemicals, and fat. Local foods conform to seasons and can be picked at peak ripeness and nutritional value, and meat can be raised on pastures rather than feed lots. But this is an argument to shop carefully rather than to rigidly avoid anything but local foods. In the end, the argument for locavorism in the United States comes down simply to taste and the benefits of knowing where your food comes from—the sense of community that comes from sharing in the production and consumption of food. But as I noted above, the undeniable appeal of fresh ingredients will have to compete with other equally compelling, aesthetic dimensions of food, some of which involve foods from distant lands.

If moral or political claims about new ways of eating cannot be sustained, where is the potential for social change in the locavore movement and modernist cuisine? There is some reason to be skeptical of both movements as agents of change. The concoctions of modernist cuisine are so unfamiliar that when people tire of the novelty it may go the way of the avant-garde in the visual arts and music—an important academic influence but not something people make part of their lives. Just as avant-garde music never gave audiences the kind of satisfaction they sought from music, modernist cuisine may not satisfy our need for familiarity in the foods we eat. The Slow Food/heritage/locavore movement may also be just another fad to be cast aside when foodies find some other bright, shiny object to chase. If the Slow Food/heritage/locavore movement understands food traditions as too static, and thus lacking in creative innovation, it may go the way of other traditions that have failed to keep up with the pace of social change.

Nevertheless, despite these reservations, I think this skepticism is unwarranted because both movements so clearly and deeply represent opposing forces in culture, forces that reflect a conflict, not just about aesthetic judgments but also about ways of life, styles of thought, and the fate of generations. These two movements taken together embody the extraordinary conflict between technology and nature that influences almost every dimension of modern life. As technology takes over more and more of our world, the theme of whither nature and the goal of protecting its vestiges (even if highly cultivated) will be with us all the while. The activity of feeding ourselves is perhaps the most salient site of this conflict because no other activity is so basic to our material existence. Since this struggle is unlikely to be resolved soon, the alternatives offered by Slow Food/locavorism and modernist cuisine will remain live options in terms of which this larger battle is fought.

WHEN THE USELESS BECOMES BEWITCHING

The Slow Food movement and modernist cuisine appear, on the surface, to be quite opposed to each other. One represents the resistance of our food traditions to the march of technological innovation. The other represents the leading edge of that march. I hope to show that this conflict between these movements is more apparent than real and that, at a deeper level, they represent complementary trends in a society desperately seeking relief from a dehumanized world.

This conflict between technology and those who resist it is, in part, about the role of instrumental reason, or, to put it more simply, our excessive reliance on efficiency as a foundational value. The Slow Food movement, with its relaxed rhythms and adherence to tradition, ignores the value of efficiency. The point of eating is to savor the moment without the crush of schedules and external demands on our time and attention. By contrast, modernist cuisine seeks more efficient technological mechanisms for extracting more flavor, while dispensing with the old, less efficient methods, and thus it embodies the essence of instrumental reason. However, this appearance of conflict belies a deeper and more significant similarity between these two movements. When we understand these movements correctly, we may see both as a kind of antidote to the destructive march of instrumental reason. In the end, both of these movements are about aesthetics—about enhancing the enjoyment of our sensory experience.

Aesthetics is the part of life that most easily escapes the clutches of instrumental reason. When we enjoy something for its aesthetic value, its function fades in importance and its efficiency is usually irrelevant. We enjoy a work's appearance regardless of whether it has a function. Through being wholly absorbed in the object itself, art removes us, if only for a few moments, from the dominance of instrumental value and allows us to see an object or activity as having intrinsic value, as having its end in itself, instead of having value merely as a means to something else. Through continual exposure to aesthetic objects, we experience the enriching stability and persistent meaningfulness of a world in which some objects and activities call us to undivided and unconditional commitment, an entryway into a world infused with ultimate cares, where the simple delight in something has all the meaning one could want.[7]

A sense of wonder underwrites this undivided commitment. When we recognize that an object has value beyond its usefulness or function, we become more attuned to the allusive meanings and hidden dimensions of it. We are open to the possibility of multiple interpretations and the inexhaustible mystery of things, and we confront a reality that resists our attempts to fully understand it. As the philosopher Martin Heidegger repeatedly noted, in the production of art, reality withholds something from us, escapes our attempts to control it, and is thus a source of persistent, reoccurring intrigue and fascination. Instrumental reason buries this fascination because it encourages us to believe that the function of an object and our ability to control it exhausts its value, thus evacuating it of all mystery.

Art reminds us that we can never thoroughly master reality. It always means more than what can be said and is capable of taking on forms never previously imagined, piquing our curiosity again and again, reveling in the sheer wonder at the infinite complexity of the world. Through art we embrace our limits even while we push against them, and the material world takes a stand against complete intelligibility. All art is a vain and pointless struggle against the recalcitrance of the world, which makes its resistance felt in the struggle of the artist to impose form on it.

We can never rid ourselves of instrumental reason or the value of efficiency, nor should we. It is a rational response to human vulnerability, and has brought about much good. But the moments in which we grasp the intrinsic, noninstrumental value of things are not only moments of pleasure but also moments in which we glimpse a much different sort of world, one in which matter resists conceptualization, the hard surfaces of reality resist manipulation because they have their own capacities and developmental direction, and meaning expands beyond what can be calculated or measured. It is through the recognition of intrinsic value that reality comes to have the depth that sustains commitment and motivates genuine care, a point for which I will argue more thoroughly in chapter 5 when we look at the nature of beauty.

If this account of the value of art is correct, contemporary trends in food and wine have a similar appeal. The Slow Food/heritage/locavore movements (of which the natural wine movement is a part) acknowledge and demand that we live within the constraints of the constant and insurmountable rhythm of the seasons, the vagaries of climate and weather, and other threats that make farming hazardous and uncertain. The resistance of the world is inscribed in the flavors that reflect the unique qualities of geographical locations (*terroir*), the impact of weather on ripeness, and influence of climate and soil on the availability of food, all factors over which we had very limited control until the advent of modern technology. The demand to slow down and savor opens a time and space in which we can be receptive to multiple interpretations and sense the gleam of nature in its interplay with culture that is the transformation of raw materials into a meal.

But how does modernist cuisine fit this story about the limits of our control over nature? Isn't molecular gastronomy attempting to overcome this resistance of nature to our designs? By manipulating chemical structure using the devices and techniques of modernist cuisine, food is less and less a natural object and increasingly an example of our dominance over nature. The tension between our ability to impose our will on reality and the resistance of reality to our will is right there on the plate. Do we best confront human vulnerability by preserving the past and local traditions as the Slow Food movement wishes or by changing the future as modernist cuisine advocates? The answers to life's deepest questions lie buried in the mashed potatoes.

To answer this question, we need to explore how art in general and the food movement in particular can induce social change. Many works of art explicitly take up political themes or show examples of oppression or liberation. Picasso's *Guernica*, the film *Brokeback Mountain*, or novels about the Holocaust are obvious examples. No doubt these works are inspiring, but I doubt that these depictions by themselves alter political events or provide us with new information about the events depicted. Instead, art operates more subtly behind the scenes, redefining what can be seen or said, who is visible and who is not. Questions about political participation involve decisions about what will count as speech and what is just noise. As French philosopher Jacques Rancière writes, "Politics is primarily conflict over the existence of a common stage and over the existence and status of those present on it."[8] What matters is who gets to speak. Artists give voice to people or ideas that have been marginalized. They keep memories alive, juxtapose incongruous images and make the juxtaposition seem natural, and tell stories about characters we have never met. We learn nothing new about the destruction of war from *Guernica*. But Picasso's depiction of the horror of nationalist violence during the Spanish Civil War gives representation to the victims, primarily women and children, who otherwise would have disappeared from history. Art contradicts violence by abrogating the silence of its victims.

Art also provides a space in which new characters appear and are juxtaposed with the old characters and thus achieve an equality of appearance. Through the production and consumption of art, individuals change their representations within society because art defines ways of being together or being apart, of being inside or outside, in front of or in the middle of, and changes our assumptions about who or what belongs in the same space. Warhol placed an ordinary commodity, Brillo boxes, in an art museum; *Brokeback Mountain* placed and celebrated gay relationships within the macho world of the cowboy; the Stones juxtaposed rebellion and lascivious pleasure. Art expresses the idea that we need not endorse the identities forced upon us by the authorities by reordering the occupants of the space around us. Rancière calls this the "partition of the sensible."[9] Artistic practices take part in the partition of the sensible insofar as they suspend the ordinary coordinates of sensory experience and reframe the network of social relationships we engage in by situating them in a different space and time, and by revising our perceptions of what is common and what is singular. The emergence of rock music in the 1960s performed many of these strange juxtapositions. The idea of a guitar hero is conceptually absurd. Yet, by embodying the militaristic, sacrificial idea of "hero" in the vain, individualistic posing of the rock guitarist, the idea that self-expression represents our deepest yearnings is placed on the cultural stage alongside religious devotion and corporate climbing. The volume at which rock music was played constructed a physical barrier that regulated the space around the emerging "hippie" community and drew a boundary across which complacency and conformism could not travel, while psychedelia threw open the vast fluidity of internal consciousness and put it on the public stage, the inside becoming outside. Aesthetic experience allows unconventional meanings and directions to emerge not by carrying messages but by reordering sensory experience.

In contemporary society, food plays a similar role. However, the partition of the sensible with regard to food reorders our sense of both time and space. In the first instance, it puts our lives outside the time frame of the production paradigm's emphasis on efficiency. The production paradigm prescribes a certain use of our time—the hamster wheel of production and quantitative consumption that drives the frantic pace of modern life. By contrast, the Italian meal and, more generally, locavorism make visible the human in a world of corporations and prescribes a different use of our time—the time to savor the tissue of little things that sustains life's meaning. Industrial food sends the message that there is no time for cooking or human contact, and it makes possible the opportunity to fill the day with other more "productive" activities, thus reinforcing the lack of time. It's all about the speed up, reinforcing an industrial rhythm that will sell more products. The modern mechanisms of control work by controlling how time is perceived. Because food is so central to the organization of life, via the culture of the table that control is thwarted by disrupting our sense of time.

However, time is not the only factor of production disrupted by the food revolution. By focusing on taste and hospitality we are placed outside the space of the production paradigm and its attempt to objectify persons. The production paradigm pits one person against another in a competitive space with a strict hierarchy in which sharing goes in one direction—to the top of the organization. It is inherently authoritarian. The space of hospitality with food at its center operates differently. There is a hierarchy, the carer and the cared for, but relations of reciprocity and interchange are at its core, as described in chapter 1.

The Italian meal as imagined above is idealized, to be sure. It is not an everyday occurrence and surely not a part of every Italian citizen's life. It is only one aspect of a complex culture, an abstraction we have sacralized as one example of the foodies' temple.[10] Indeed, with the traditional Italian meal we have turned life into art. The enjoyment is not merely of the sensory properties of the food but also of the meaning of a way of life. The mythology, the romance, is precisely the point.

Because the art of the Italian meal is a separate form of experience, distinct from the culture of the production paradigm and the frantic rhythms of everyday life, it is not beholden to the hierarchies that constitute society. This separateness is an elaboration of a "new" form—not an actual disconnection from the community but a tension with the status quo via the use of a mythology. Art in this case suppresses its own autonomy and identifies with the mythology. Political change, after all, must not be merely sectarian but must be working toward a good life, its *telos* must be human happiness and the enjoyment of pleasure, and so these ideals are crucial. The appeal to tradition does refer to the past but not in the name of a status quo or deference to the authority of entrenched interests. It is opposed to the dominant trends in society that run roughshod over the values of place, particularity, and tranquility.

Yet, although art and life overlap, they must remain distinct if art is to provide a critique of life. If the distinction between art and life is collapsed, it will deprive aesthetic experience of its capacity to be a center of controversy and conflict. When we suppress the boundaries of art then anything can be art, as Warhol shows with his Brillo boxes. But when art becomes too closely identified with the everyday and its deeply ingrained habits, it no longer has the capacity to surprise. It will lack the allure and enchantment that is at the essence of art. Part of the function of art is to preserve the variety of possible sensory experiences so they can't become routine, homogeneous, or ordinary. Thus, locavorism and the mythology of the Italian meal, which stand in here as symbols for all the sacred, traditional spaces of the food world, are not sufficient to sustain a revolution. They are always in danger of stultification, of becoming safe and pat, and worse, of being absorbed into the mainstream. If art is to be constantly updating its revolutionary role, it must remain in tension with the everyday. This is the role of modernist cuisine. Every revolutionary art needs an outside, something to unsettle the dominant forms of social change to prevent it from becoming mere repetition. Thus, in order for the food revolution to succeed, there must be constant tension between the tradition-bound, parochial, conservatism of the Slow Food/locavore movement and the innovation of modernist cuisine. The Italian meal is one sensory world; modernist cuisine quite another. It's the tension between the two that explains food's revolutionary promise.

How does the sensory conflict engage political energies? This issue is one that has dogged philosophical views advocating the revolutionary potential of art from Schiller to Adorno. In the case of food, however, there is a ready answer—by preserving the interest in taste as an adventure—which, as I argue in the final chapter of this book, cannot easily be assimilated to corporate interests. Locavorism provokes a break with industrial food production. But what that enables us to see is a world of flavor in the thrall of subjectivity and play. When the world of pleasure is disconnected from the production paradigm and creates its own community at least the potential for social change exists.

Thus, both the Slow Food/locavore movement and modernist cuisine, despite their opposition, have something in common. They both direct our attention to the realm of the aesthetic where we least expect to find it—in the pleasures and joys of everyday life. Therein lay their true value.

Philosophers have long considered wine and food to be too related to a function or purpose to have intrinsic value. But the fact that we eat food to satisfy nutritional requirements and drink wine to enjoy the effects of alcohol does not preclude them from having intrinsic value as well—in the absence of hunger or any desire to be inebriated, food and wine can be enjoyed for purely aesthetic reasons. The peculiar potency of wine and food as works of art lies in the fact that they are accessible to us every day. Much of day-to-day life revolves around securing, preparing, and consuming food. Thus, wine and food are commonplace enough to express the quality of ordinary life. However, when we focus on their aesthetic dimension, they achieve some distance from their practical function and need not succumb to the deadening effects of instrumental reason. Wine and food, when considered aesthetically, bring traces of the sacred to people otherwise thoroughly enmeshed in instrumental value.

Great art reveals the inexhaustible beauty of the world. But this can be experienced much more readily in a practical engagement with reality, in something as ordinary as the consumption of food or wine, rather than the abstract space of the museum or the symphony hall. The Slow Food movement is not a solution to our problems of sustainability. It is instead a call to find something sacred in our lives, something that has intrinsic value. Similarly, modernist cuisine is not merely a set of tools and practices for becoming more efficient in the kitchen. It is an attempt to make eating mysterious and intriguing and to discover sheer moments of joy in the fantastic concoctions of these remarkably creative chefs.

The aesthetic world of food and beverage—a community of taste—is the primary site of resistance, in the modern world, to the inexorable colonization of reality by instrumental reason. It remains to be seen whether this is a gathering of the tribes or a passing fad to be swept up in the rise of the machines. It is, in any case, a silent revolt that quietly cultivates the thin reed of a human kind of flourishing in the muddy bog of a dehumanized world.

It is these glimpses of the sacred in the everyday that really make life meaningful. The revolution in taste is a revolution in the tissue of little things that hold life together, which may never make the history books, but makes individual lives immeasurably better. By transforming the commonplace, art, especially the edible arts, reinforces the sacred in the profane and suffuses life with an aura of mystery visible only when the useless becomes bewitching.

4

FROM PLEASURE TO BEAUTY

If Kant Was at Myhrvold's Table

Not everyone is on board with the food revolution. The backlash in the media has been strident and dismissive. Steve Poole, author of *You Aren't What You Eat: Fed Up with Gastroculture*, has led the charge. Using terms like "emotional derangement" and "food psychosis" to describe our current fascination with food, Poole's writings on the subject are long on rhetoric and short on argument. He writes, "But to suppose that eating can nourish the spirit looks like a category mistake: just the sort of category mistake that led the early church to define 'gluttony' as a sin," before he goes on to endorse the early church's view that gluttony (defined as an excessive preoccupation with food) is a sin. Why it is a sin we are never told. Instead, we get confident assertions such as "It should be obvious that a steak is not like a symphony, a pie not like a passacaglia, foie gras not like a fugue; that the 'composition' of a menu is not like the composition of a requiem; that the cook heating things in the kitchen and arranging them on a plate is not the artistic equal of Charlie Parker."[1] But of course the whole premise of his diatribe is that this is not obvious to countless people who otherwise seem quite sane.

It would be nice if he would let us in on his reasons for dismissing the interests of what he prefers to call "foodists." But instead he gives us florid descriptions of menu items in restaurants and evidence that our judgments about food are often influenced by our beliefs about what we're eating—as if judgments about art, music, and anything else are not influenced by beliefs. In the end we are left with platitudes. "Might it not, after all, be a good idea to worry more about what we put into our minds than what we put into our mouths?" he asks, without explaining how my love for a good daube somehow makes me incapable of distinguishing sense from nonsense.

Despite the cheap rhetoric, it is not hard to discern Poole's point. He thinks people who take an "excessive" interest in food are light-minded and unserious. Food, according to him, is pleasurable but insignificant, and the kind of pleasure it produces is inconsequential and lacking in depth. After we fill our bellies and gain a few moments of enjoyment, we should move on to more important matters. This dismissive attitude toward sensory pleasure has a respectable pedigree. Among philosophers who have thought about art and aesthetics, the status of food and wine has been tenuous at best. Food and wine receive little discussion in their work compared to painting or music, and when food and wine are discussed, most philosophers are skeptical that they belong in the category of fine art.[2] It is alleged that the pleasures of food are neither deeply felt nor genuinely moving; they are based on fleeting, constantly changing desires that lack stability and permanence and are subject to fads and fashion, a distracting substitute for real satisfactions that come from the appreciation of the fine arts that have stood the test of time like literature or painting. Furthermore, it is argued, the appreciation of food is effortless, passive consumption requiring nothing more than a biological capacity for discernment rather than intellectually focused attention or serious thought. In the end, food is thought to give us only simple pleasures associated with our animal nature and the "low-information" senses of taste and smell and is thus not worthy of serious study. The term "foodie," with its connotation of something small, cute, and insignificant, seems to embody all these assumptions.

Piled on top of these accusations is the notion encouraged by social theorists such as Pierre Bourdieu that an appreciation of fine food is nothing but a marker and signal of superior social status.[3] Yet chefs such as Ferran Adrià and Nathan Myhrvold insist that some culinary creations are works of art. As Myhrvold, author of the monumental cooking text *Modernist Cuisine* writes in his seminal essay "The Art in Gastronomy: A Modernist Perspective," "Food can engage our senses, our minds, and our emotions just as profoundly as carefully chosen words or brush strokes. Arguably, our relation with food is even more intimate because we consume it directly. So there is no fundamental reason that food cannot be art—it has all the right prerequisites."[4]

Is this "art envy" just a conceit of celebrity chefs with inflated egos? Or are we witnessing the birth of a new art form delivered by the development of molecular gastronomy and encouraged by armies of "foodies" chasing the perfect bite? I think food (and wine) can be art if conceptualized properly. But the skeptics, doubtful that something as ordinary as food could be art, must first have their say before we can bring the edible arts into focus.[5]

In previous chapters, I've argued that the pleasure we get from food has some special characteristics that distinguish it from other pleasures. The pleasures of the table play a central role in ordinary life and the "tissue of little things" that infuse life with meaning. As important as these pleasures may be in everyday life, it might be argued, they are nevertheless not something profound or possessed of deep meaning. It may be that the cognitive dimensions of food and beverage are too thin to provide us with robust aesthetic experiences. Sensory experience is one thing, intellectual stimulation quite another, and perhaps food doesn't provide us with the kinds of intellectual stimulation and cognitive rewards that music, painting, or literature provide. The philosophical arguments supporting the backlash against the food revolution are serious, and so we must take them into account and show where they go wrong, if in fact they do go wrong.

Despite the lack of interest in food matters among contemporary philosophers, food and wine have not always been marginalized in discussions of aesthetics. In the eighteenth century, taste provided a model for how to understand aesthetic judgments in general—until Kant came along to break up the party. Immanuel Kant, the great eighteenth-century German philosopher, looms like Goliath over modern philosophy, and inquiry in aesthetics is no exception. Kant argued that food and wine could not be genuine aesthetic objects and his considerable influence has carried the day and continues to influence philosophical thinking about the arts. Most of the above mentioned objections stem from adopting a Kantian approach to aesthetics, and so I will go straight to the "horse's mouth" and explore Kant's view.

Kant acknowledges the obvious point that judgments regarding "mouth taste" as well as the genuine aesthetic appreciation of paintings, music, and literature are based on an individual's subjective experience of pleasure. But with "mouth taste" there is no reflection or imagination involved, just an immediate response. The pleasure comes first, and then we judge, based on the amount of pleasure experienced, whether we find the flavors "agreeable" or "disagreeable." Thus, our judgments about food and wine are based entirely on our subjective, idiosyncratic, personal, sensuous preferences. For Kant, good food is pleasing, but it can never be beautiful—it can never have genuine aesthetic value. By contrast, when we experience paintings or music aesthetically, contemplation ensues whereby our rational and imaginative capacities are engaged. Our pleasure is not an immediate response to the object but comes after the contemplation. We respond not only to whether the object is pleasing but also to how the object engages our cognitive capacities of understanding and imagination. This yields a judgment that is based on more than a mere subjective preference; it is based on a universal form of appreciation in which we judge the object to be beautiful. Because we enjoy food without having to think about the enjoyment, food offers only a limited form of sensuous pleasure without the intellectual engagement that contributes to our enjoyment of the fine arts.

Kant was wrong to argue that "mouth taste" does not provoke contemplation or intellectual engagement. Connoisseurs of wine, cheese, coffee, and beer, as well as the flavorists who analyze our food preferences for the food industry, and countless chefs who study flavor pairing show that food and wine can be thoughtfully savored, and various components of the tasting experience can be analyzed. In fact, the smell of a richly flavored soup is more like an idea than a sensation. The ingredients stimulate hundreds of different types of receptors that line the nose, and the mind binds these sensations into a single aroma, which an experienced taster can analyze into parts. But these aromas are then interpreted using contextual clues that allow us to make a judgment about what we are tasting, leaving us open to the power of suggestion—how a food is labeled, the beliefs we have about an object, and our past experience with it can profoundly influence what we smell and taste. We subjectively get more pleasure from wine and food marked as expensive or a common piece of meat that is labeled with a fancy name. Taste is a complex idea that implicates our cognitive capacities, not a simple, passively experienced sensation.

But these facts by themselves don't refute Kant's view. What mattered for Kant was not the mere fact of contemplation, but rather how the contemplation unfolds and what its result is. So we have to look more closely at what Kant had in mind. What does the contemplation of painting or music supply that cannot be accomplished by savoring food? According to Kant, the proper contemplation of painting, music, or literature (1) results in disinterested satisfaction and (2) must involve the "free play" of the imagination and the understanding. Like the pleasure we get from "mouth taste," we get pleasure from the contemplation of a painting. But genuine aesthetic pleasure is not based on any interest we have in the object—the object's usefulness, ability to serve our needs, or prospects for earning a profit are not part of the experience. Instead, according to Kant, we revel in the pure appearance of the object because we have no interest in what it can do for us, aside from giving us pleasure. Of course, we can have a financial interest in a painting or an emotional connection to a play written by a friend, but then our experience is no longer genuinely aesthetic. In genuine aesthetic experience our pleasure does not rest on satisfying a desire. Once we are free of the distracting influence of desire, we can contemplate how the object stimulates the interplay of imagination and understanding that gives rise to a disinterested form of pleasure or satisfaction. Food, by contrast, is appreciated because it relieves hunger or entertains guests. Its appreciation is inherently bound up with a practical purpose that requires the satisfaction of a desire and is thus not disinterested.

This also means that art, music, and literature, unlike food, engage our critical faculties. Because our judgments about art can be disinterested and because we all share the faculties of the imagination and understanding, we are justified in expecting others to find the object pleasing as well. We think that others should agree with our subjective judgments, although we may realize that such agreement is unlikely. Thus, our judgments regarding the beauty of art or music, because they do not rest on personal, idiosyncratic desires, are capable of being communicated to others; they aspire to be universal, although Kant insists there is no rule or way of proving via argument that an object is beautiful.

The problem with "mouth taste" is that it is inherently linked to desire and personal preference, and is thus never disinterested. Judgments about art are subject to criticism because they aspire to be universal whereas judgments about food are not. If a person fails to like chocolate, they cannot be criticized for that failure; by contrast, if they fail to like Rembrandt's paintings, they can be criticized for lack of aesthetic sensitivity.

In summary, for Kant, the first step in moving from pleasure to beauty is to see an object for what it is independently of its function, as if it served no purpose other than as an object of pure, aesthetic contemplation. However, it is puzzling that Kant failed to notice that food or wine could be consumed purely for the aesthetic pleasure they produce. Although food satisfies hunger, it needn't always be used for that purpose. The fact that something has instrumental value does not logically preclude it from having intrinsic value in the right context. A piece of ancient pottery may have been useful for holding liquid, but its usefulness as a container need not enter into a judgment regarding its aesthetic value. A painting may be used merely as decoration, but that doesn't preclude the aesthetic appreciation of it. In fact, the argument seems to be applied selectively. Architecture has long been considered a fine art despite its obvious connection to the function of buildings. Until roughly the eighteenth century, people did not sit raptly before a group of musicians contemplating sounds as aesthetic objects only. Music has always played a functional role within ceremonies or as a stimulus for dancing or socializing. Today, arguably, music is primarily used as a mood regulator or as background to provide atmosphere. Yet the fact that music and architecture are useful for some purpose does not prevent them from being enjoyed as aesthetic objects under the appropriate conditions.

Why should food be different? Obviously, we regularly eat because we're hungry, and hunger may unduly influence our judgments about flavor. So have a snack. Once we are no longer ravenous, there is no reason to think judgments about flavors will be distorted or excessively "interested." We can then focus on aesthetic properties just as we can enjoy the beauty of a building without worrying about whether it will withstand earthquakes. Of course, there are biological and cultural differences between us that sometimes prevent us from agreeing about matters of taste. But there are cultural and personal differences between art critics that prevent them from finding agreement about paintings. Disagreement among critics does not disqualify painting and music from being works of art, nor should it disqualify food and wine. We do not practice the culture of the table merely in order to relieve our hunger. Kant got this wrong. So food and wine experiences can have intrinsic value—they are valuable in themselves, not because of some additional purpose they serve.

In fact, Kant's claim that genuine aesthetic appreciation must be free of any taint of desire seems wholly misguided. Many critics of Kant have pointed to difficulties in understanding how taking pleasure in the way an object engages one's imagination could be disinterested. If something causes pleasure, don't I have an interest in experiencing it again? Why doesn't taking pleasure in a beautiful painting produce a desire to experience the object again?

These worries point to a deeper problem that is fatal to Kant's view that genuine aesthetic experience must be free of desire. The most plausible contemporary account of desire is provided by Timothy Schroeder, who develops a view of desire and pleasure that incorporates what contemporary neuroscience has to say on the subject. In the course of analyzing the nature of desire he defines pleasure as follows: "To be pleased is (at least) to represent a net increase in desire satisfaction relative to expectation."[6] For my purposes, Schroeder's key claim is that the pleasure centers of the brain are intrinsically tied to our motivational states—that is, desires. In other words, there is no such thing as a pleasure that is not dependent on a desire. Pleasure just is a representation of a change in desire satisfaction—pleasure is the mechanism through which we come to know a desire has been satisfied. Thus, according to the best evidence we have, there is no such thing as a disinterested pleasure. Kantian aesthetics rests on a fiction. Thus, Kant's distinction between taking pleasure in food because it satisfies a desire and taking disinterested pleasure in a painting because desires are not engaged simply will not withstand scrutiny. Any activity we undertake, if it produces pleasure, will require that a desire be satisfied. Thus Kant's argument that there is a fundamental difference between "mouth taste" and disinterested aesthetic experience collapses.

However, even if this argument is successful and the appreciation of food does have intrinsic value independent of any purpose it might serve, there is a further question about what kind of intrinsic value the experience of food has. Is a good meal valuable in the way a warming sun or a massage are valuable—as momentary sources of sensory pleasure? Or is the satisfaction we get from food and wine of a more profound sort more closely associated with art appreciation? It may be that the second dimension of Kant's theory—contemplation based on the "free play of understanding and imagination"—might give us some reason to maintain Kant's view of the inferiority of mouth taste as an object of genuine aesthetic appreciation. But what is this "play of understanding and imagination," and does that apply to food and wine?

According to Kant, through experience the mind naturally builds up a collection of schemata—templates for various kinds of objects—that help us recognize a dog as a dog or a table as a table. When we encounter an object, it is the imagination that selects and structures sensory data so that it matches these templates according to what is the best fit. New experiences of dogs and tables can thus be easily assimilated to our conceptual scheme via the understanding and we can then recognize the object as a dog or table. However, we are not born with all the templates we need for understanding reality—we have to create new ones when we encounter new objects. So the imagination also has the ability to sort through sensory experience and invent new templates. When doing so, the imagination cannot simply apply the old templates since they don't fit the new experience very well. But the imagination can still make use of them if they are sufficiently close to the new experience. This is what Kant means by the "free play" of the imagination and understanding. The imagination is searching for a concept to fit the new experience, but to find a match it has to shape the sensory data to fit existing concepts in the understanding as best it can, while also shaping existing concepts so they match the new sensory data. An example might help make this clear. Consider the statement "true love isn't fickle." To grasp this statement, we take the concept "love" and see it as having the property of steadfastness—genuine love doesn't come and go easily. But in the hands of Shakespeare, this ordinary statement becomes a thing of beauty:

> Love is not love
> Which alters as it alteration finds,
> Or bends with the remover to remove:
> O, no! it is an ever-fixed mark,
> That looks on tempests and is never shaken;
> It is the star to every wandering bark,
> Whose worth's unknown, although his height be taken.
> Love's not Time's fool, though rosy lips and cheeks
> Within his bending sickle's compass come;
> Love alters not with his brief hours and weeks,
> But bears it out even to the edge of doom. [7]

In a sense, the Shakespeare sonnet is simply categorizing love as among those things that don't change rapidly. But the words trigger a barrage of thoughts and associations—love isn't just steadfast but steadfast in times of great need; in the face of overwhelming circumstances, it is not merely relatively unchanging but can remain steadfast to the "edge of doom." This is the imagination at play, pushing back against the too literal work of the understanding. Love is not steadfast in an ordinary way but in particular circumstances can be quite extraordinary.

In this exercise of the imagination, we may succeed or fail. There may not be a concept or schema adequate to the new experience. It may elude our understanding if the object is sufficiently alien to our conceptual framework.

This free play of the imagination and understanding is the key to understanding our aesthetic judgments, according to Kant. In a genuine aesthetic judgment, rather than a mere sensuously enjoyable experience like basking in the sun, or in Kant's view, sipping wine, the imagination experiments with possible ways of restructuring the object. This is what we do when we try to grasp what Shakespeare means when he describes the stability of love in terms of these elaborate metaphors.

It is this searching activity that we find enjoyable, especially when that restructuring makes sense to us, when the understanding and the imagination finally harmonize despite the fact that the imagination is not being thoroughly directed by the fixed templates that normally govern our concepts. We see that the work has an order and unity to it without clearly deciding on a single judgment of what it is or what it does. There is no concept adequate to the experience—in other contexts steadfastness must be differently described—but that indeterminacy is itself pleasurable. This is when we judge an object beautiful. It is intriguing, mysterious, not fully understood, yet at the same time balanced, harmonious, and well put together. Shakespeare's sonnet raises all kinds of questions about love's steadfastness—of course we all know love can sometimes be as fickle as spring weather. It is this experience of a concept pushed to its limit that we find enjoyable. Thus, an aesthetic judgment is not based on the object, as much as it is based on our reaction to our reflection on the object. In this second dimension of Kant's view, we move from pleasure to the recognition of beauty by imaginatively grasping the subtle, surprising, ambiguous effects of an object as they expand our understanding of it.

Kant's discussion of the free play of imagination and understanding is both interesting and compelling. However, I doubt that this account of aesthetic pleasure explains all genuine aesthetic judgments—it seems too remote from the sensuous experiences we typically associate with the appreciation of art, especially music. It is not obvious that all genuine appreciation of music involves an indeterminate search for understanding. Listening to music is not like solving a puzzle. But Kant's theory captures some of our aesthetic judgments. The question is whether the appreciation of food and wine ever takes this form. And I think it clearly does. This kind of indeterminate play between our concept of what something is and an intriguing, sensuous experience that we cannot quite place in any traditional category is precisely the aim of modernist cuisine. The moments of uncertainty and surprise and the deconstructive gestures of these dishes aim to provoke the kind of intellectual playfulness that Kant thought was the essence of aesthetic experience. When the flavors are genuinely delicious and we experience the harmony and unity of the flavor profile along with the intellectual pleasures of searching for indeterminate meaning, a judgment that the object is beautiful seems appropriate. Caviar made from sodium alginate and calcium, burning sherbets, and spaghetti made from vegetables produce precisely this kind of response. They challenge the intellect and force our imagination to restructure our conceptual framework, just as Kant suggested. But even traditional cooking, if it is sufficiently creative and innovative, can produce this enjoyable experience of indeterminate searching, as we strive to place a dish in its appropriate tradition.

Wine tasting also depends on the play of understanding and imagination. As the very literate wine importer Terry Theise writes,

> I can scarcely recall a great wine that didn't in some sense amaze me, that didn't make my palate feel as if it were whipsawed between things that hardly ever travel together. My shorthand term for that experience is paradox; again, this component is in the hands of the angels and doesn't appear susceptible to human contrivance, but when it is found it conveys a lovely sense of wonder: How can these things coexist in a single wine? And not only coexist, but spur each other on; power with grace, depth with brilliance. [8]

That is a lovely description of the play of understanding and imagination as Theise struggles to understand how the wine can have contradictory properties. Kant was right to point to this kind of experience as a genuinely aesthetic experience but wrong in his judgment that food or wine could not generate it. One wonders what the old professor, who allegedly never ventured more than ten miles from his home in Königsberg, had on his plate for dinner. If Kant were at Mhyrvold's table, he might indeed have fallen in love. After all, he was reputed to have a taste for the grape; perhaps his dismissive attitude tells us something about the quality of eighteenth-century wine.

I have been considering Kant's view in some detail because it is important to show that mouth taste has the depth to be considered genuinely beautiful in the same way that works of art and music can be beautiful. But while I agree with Kant that beauty has depth, I disagree with the way he seems to push sensory experience aside in favor of an excessively intellectual account of aesthetic experience. For Kant, it is intellectual sense-making activity that we find pleasurable, not complex sensory experience itself. But Kant's view is too limited to explain the appeal of painting and music, let alone food and wine, when we focus on the enjoyment of the sensory surface of the work, without engaging in this intellectual game of trying to categorize where it fits. Most art has an irreducible sensory dimension that is essential to our appreciation of it, and this sensory dimension is crucial to art's ability to engage our reason. The lovely textures of Claude Debussy's tone poem *La Mer* engage our attention regardless of whether we follow his directive to consider it a representation of our experience of the sea. The low-level dread that infuses the dynamic, layered meanderings of Radiohead gets under your skin long before their paradoxical love/hate relationship with the technological dreamscape comes into conceptual focus.

This sensuous dimension of art is significant because our appreciation of food surely depends on how it tastes. Food and wine are among the most sensuous of the arts—it's the sensory enjoyment that provokes wonder and leads to contemplation, and sensory enjoyment remains the focus of that wonder. We might enjoy the way food engages our imagination, but that cognitive enjoyment in no way leaves sensual pleasure behind. Aesthetic judgments can take the form Kant prescribes, and so can our judgments about food. But this cognitive enjoyment is not a sufficient condition for the distinctive kind of aesthetic pleasure characteristic of mouth taste. Food can make us think, but it must taste good if it is to provide us with an aesthetic experience.

In summary, there is no philosophical basis for claiming that the pleasures of food are unable to engage our rational capacities or that we are precluded from finding intellectual pleasure in food. Its unrelenting sensuous dimension does not make an interest in food superficial or merely functional. But more must be said about how food engages our intellect and how it acquires the depth of meaning that makes it worthy of being considered a fine art.

SENSUALITY AND ART

"Live in the moment" has been the advice of sensualists from Epicurus to Camus. Peak experiences, moments of extreme pleasure, or catalyzing emotion, can nourish life, especially when not burdened with a guilty past or an anxious future. Wine lovers and gastrophiles are sensualists, or at least we strive to be when the cares of everyday life are not too pressing. But this advice to live in the moment seldom comes with a set of instructions for how we should do it. It is not easy, and for genuine sensualists "living (only) in the moment" is a bad idea. We are all familiar with the shallow sensualists chasing after any source of stimulation with no thought of the future or the past. For the Jay Gatsbys of the world, it usually ends badly. But in addition to being a road to ruin, shallow sensations won't produce a peak experience. Finding peak experiences requires commitment over the long term. You first of all must find out what you like. That requires introspection and a confrontation with one's own demons, weaknesses, and curmudgeonly ogres who like to stamp out the green shoots of pleasure before they bloom. Once you discover what you like, you then have to make it persistently part of your life if it is to be satisfying. That means figuring out why you like it, so you can recognize other things that might produce the same response. Our senses must be trained to notice quality lest we miss opportunities to discover it. Finally, the genuine sensualist must learn how to acquire or create what she likes to insure demand does not outstrip supply. A successful life devoted to sensual pleasure is hard work.

Most important, genuine sensuality involves the desire to explore. Real beauty is always accompanied by the sense that there are hidden depths in the admired object, something lurking just beyond the horizon of "now," a promise that only the future can keep. This sense of wonder or rapt curiosity is itself a sensual experience that boosts the dopamine deluge and makes the experience extraordinary. Pleasure is a means to further exploration; the experience of beauty produces a desire for more beauty. To genuinely "live in the moment," to squeeze everything that the moment has to offer, is to be projected into the future on the wings of one's curiosity.

But this curiosity and sense of wonder knows no temporal or spatial boundaries. Everything has an origin. A flavor is not just a flavor but a flavor pregnant with meaning traceable back to people, places, communities, and traditions. In the moment of a taste experience, we are connected to a world around us, one that existed prior to our own existence in the present. The task of gaining knowledge of origins, a place and time on which the present depends, engages the mind and unites it with the senses in a single experience. Moments, by themselves, regardless of how vivid, are too ephemeral to stitch together meaningful lives. "Living in the moment" requires the work of remembering the past and creating the future.

All works of art, if they are successful, grab our attention because they promise something more. We sense an unrealized potential for further experience, we feel our interest aroused, curiosity piqued, as if we can't quite get enough of the object. Wonder is a good way of describing that feeling of having our interest aroused. All successful art, whatever else it might accomplish, provokes wonder.[9]

Can food or beverages provoke wonder and do they express wonder? It would seem so; yet wonder is an emotion, a distinctive feeling state, and philosophers take a dim view of the capacity of food and wine to express emotion. We can be such killjoys sometimes. Here is Elizabeth Telfer in her book *Food for Thought*: "A cook can cook as an act of love, as we have seen, or out of the joy of living. But whereas in music the emotion is somehow expressed in the product itself—the music can be sad or joyful, angry or despairing—in food the emotion is only the motive behind the product."[10] And here is one of the most prominent writers on aesthetics in the twentieth century, Frank Sibley: "Perfumes and flavours, natural or artificial, are necessarily limited: unlike the major arts, they have no expressive connections with emotions, love or hate, grief, joy, terror, suffering, yearning, pity or sorrow—or with plot or character development."[11]

To understand their objections to the expressiveness of food, we have to understand how works of art in general express emotions. But that is a difficult subject. We obviously have feeling responses to art, but the mechanisms of that response are a source of significant disagreement among philosophers, as is the sense in which art objects express emotions. Narratives, songs with lyrical content, and paintings that have a narrative element often represent scenes that in real life evoke certain emotions—anger, fear, sadness, grief, and so on. However, sad songs typically don't make us feel sad; figures in paintings exhibit anger without necessarily making the viewer angry. We don't experience these emotions because the beliefs supporting sadness or anger are absent—we are not directly disappointed or offended by the events depicted in the narrative. Nevertheless, we can empathize with the characters in the narrative and feel a weakened analogue of the emotion. Many abstract paintings depict no narrative at all and so the mechanisms by which they express emotion are less then straightforward. Music, especially instrumental music that lacks lyrical content, is even more puzzling in its ability to express emotion. The conventional view of instrumental music holds that the tensions, releases, and the flow of music resemble the tension, releases, and flow of emotion. This resemblance allows us to interpret the music as embodying an emotion like sadness or love, and feel something like these emotions, although again our feeling state lacks the beliefs and thus the intensity that comes with real-life sadness and love.

Telfer and Sibley are arguing that food, unlike painting or literature, does not depict scenes to which we respond emotionally. Nor does it resemble emotions like sadness or love in the way music does, and thus it lacks the expressiveness of genuine art. No doubt food can trigger emotions in us. But, with the exception of revulsion, it seems to do so via a circuitous route. An apple pie can cause you to remember your mother who baked apple pie for your birthday and that may trigger emotional responses to the memory. But the emotion is not directed at the food; it's directed at your mother. The food is just triggering the memory. According to the conventional view, without those memories of mom, the apple pie is just a tasty dessert, apparently with no emotional overtones.

This skepticism towards food's expressiveness, however, does presuppose certain assumptions about memory that may not be warranted. Research into how memory works is still young and incomplete, but there is substantial evidence that our memories are unreliable and in fact are shaped by present events. Referring to autobiographical memories, psychologist Charles Fernyhough argues, "They are mental reconstructions, nifty multimedia collages of how things were, that are shaped by how things are now. Autobiographical memories are stitched together as and when they are needed from information stored in many different neural systems. That makes them curiously susceptible to distortion, and often not nearly as reliable as we would like."[12]

We assume that human memory functions like a computer's memory, precisely encoding information that can be accurately recalled later. But this idea was abandoned long ago by cognitive psychologists. Memory, it seems, is closer to imagination than is commonly believed. Fernyhough continues:

> The great pioneer of memory research, Daniel Schacter, has argued that, even when it is failing, memory is doing exactly what it is supposed to do. And that purpose is as much about looking into the future as it is about looking into the past. There is only a limited evolutionary advantage in being able to reminisce about what happened to you, but there is a huge payoff in being able to use that information to work out what is going to happen next. Similar neural systems seem to underpin past-related and future-related thinking. Memory is endlessly creative, and at one level it functions just as imagination does.[13]

But if this is the case, sensory experience, including present taste experience, can actively shape memories and our emotional response to memories. Your memory of mom's apple pie may be influenced as much by the apple pie in front of you and the impact of its particular flavors than by an actual memory from childhood. To the degree the experience triggers an emotional response, it is a response to an imagined version of your mom's apple pie that relies on present experience. Thus, the emotion may be "about the food" as much as it is "about your mother." Consider, for example, this dish created by Grant Achatz of Alinea:

> Achatz showed off a dish he'll be offering at the restaurant, a play on roasted marshmallows featuring sweet potatoes cooked in blue corn for a blackish, log-type hue that are then sprinkled with flavored alcoholic tapioca maltodextrin and served to the table flaming. It's served alongside another dish with housemade marshmallows. It's meant to evoke powerful memories of the past, something Achatz emphasized as an important element of the dining experience.[14]

Although the dish evokes memories of toasted marshmallows from childhood, part of the emotional response will surely be directed at the stunning presentation and juxtapositions of flavors in the dish itself. The flavors do not merely trigger the memory of an emotional response from the past; they trigger a reexperience of something like the original emotion. The flavors and textures in Achatz's dish are an imaginative representation of those flavors from the past which we perhaps experienced around a campfire when young, just as, for instance, Picasso's *Weeping Woman* is a representation of a face in the throes of war-induced grief that might cause a viewer to experience a weakened form of empathetic grief herself. Achatz's dish expresses the feelings associated with communion around a campfire just as Picasso's *Weeping Woman* expresses grief. Of course, if one lacks the experience of campfires, then Achatz's dish will just be a plate of sweet potatoes with marshmallows. But if one lacks an understanding of war-induced grief, Picasso's painting will just be a representation of an oddly shaped face. Thus, Sibley and Telfer are wrong to argue that the flavors and textures of food cannot express emotion and have no connection to narrative elements such as plot or character development. Food has a substantial capacity to express emotion and is intimately connected to a variety of characters and narratives that populate our memories.

I will argue in the next chapter that traditions are narratives and food traditions, including family traditions, are accessible via the flavors that represent those traditions. But it is worth pointing out here that the demand that art must be associated with a narrative or provide a representation of something is mistaken. There are countless successful paintings that do not tell stories or represent anything in the ordinary sense of "represent." But the main counterexample to the view that art must be representational is music. Music expresses emotion even when there are no lyrics to provide narrative context. It is a bit more complicated than this, but there are essentially two ways in which (nonnarrative) music expresses emotion. As I argued above, music can provide representations of emotion because we experience the tensions, releases, the rising and falling trajectory and intensity of music as analogous to similar patterns in various emotions. In that sense, music can, by analogy, be sad, joyful, angry, or despairing. But these are metaphorical descriptions of the music and the emotions we feel in response are at best weakened versions of those emotions; listening to sad music is often exhilarating and anything but sad. I feel genuine sadness when listening to music only if the music is bad, despairing only if it's really bad. The flavors and textures of food do not resemble emotions in this sense, although a particular dish, such as the one created by Grant Achatz (described above), can resemble flavors and textures that triggered emotions in the past.

The second way in which music expresses emotion is to directly cause it in the listener. We can be startled, surprised, calmed, or excited by music. It influences our moods by inducing cheerfulness or melancholy independently of any narrative content. The emotions we feel when listening to music are responses to sensations because they can be felt independently of whatever limited capacity music has to represent anything.[15] I would argue, in fact, that sensuous beauty itself can provoke emotions such as wonder, intrigue, excitement, pensive meditation, joy, serenity, intensity, tenderness, and so on, not because beauty reminds us of these feelings, but because it directly causes them.

As noted above, the evocation of wonder is what unites all successful art. Thus, we return to the question: Can food evoke wonder? Can the flavors and textures themselves evoke intrigue, excitement, joy, or serenity, perhaps even love? Describing his visit to a Spanish "gastro-temple" Matt Goulding writes, "The meal detonated an explosion of diverse emotions—hushed reverence, brooding reflection, fits of wonder and whimsy and piercing nostalgia—as only the very best food can. In terms of a transcendent dining experience, dinner for me at Can Roca lacked nothing."[16]

The perception of beauty in wine too evokes wonder, mystery, brooding reflection, and whimsy along with joy, anticipation, confusion, amusement, a sense of loss and impermanence, and so on. New taste sensations, exotic cuisines, and the strange concoctions of modernist cuisine produce wonder at least in culinarians who are open to exploring them as objects of fascination. Particular dishes and menus also provoke wonder about their origins and the traditions from which they emerge.

Part of the feeling of wonder is the sense that something is not fully understood. Objects that evoke wonder are perplexing or mysterious. Some wines are as mysterious and engrossing as a painting or musical work. Just as great works of art grab our attention because they promise something more, in a great wine we sense an unrealized potential for further experience, we feel our interest aroused, curiosity piqued, as if we can never quite get enough of it. Like the meal described above, they induce a sense of wonder. They silence conversation and change the mood of a room from lively, sociable chatter to wistful surrender to the sublime, a contemplative state in which the wine itself seems to probe its own nature, searching for a more discursive means of expression. The presence of contradiction and anomaly are essential to wonder, for wonder presents something that we can't quite comprehend. We are transfixed by objects that are capable of harboring incompatible qualities as Theise noted above in his response to certain wines. All of the great wines embody contradiction at their core: power and finesse, complexity and simplicity, weight and delicacy, solidity and agility. The finest wines, which are not necessarily the most expensive, are as mysterious and engrossing as a painting or musical work. They beckon as if avowing, "Make me a part of your life and I will promise eternal happiness."

KNOWLEDGE AND APPRECIATION

A great wine or meal is a sensuous storm, a blizzard of carnal confetti. But this sensuality that expresses wonder does not remain on the surface providing only deliciousness. One of the significant features of the food revolution is that we are drawn by sensory pleasure to apply our cognitive faculties. We cannot get maximum enjoyment from the sensory features of food or wine without factual knowledge about origins and the context of production. The proud display of this preoccupation with what outsiders perceive as irrelevant minutia is part of what gives foodies and wine geeks the reputation for snobbish elitism. Yet such knowledge is essential to full appreciation of food and beverages—certain pleasures are unattainable without such knowledge. Furthermore, the role of knowledge in appreciation is relevant to the question of whether cooking and winemaking are arts, because art, unlike mere entertainment, is cognitively demanding. Genuine appreciation involves knowledge of how a work of art is put together and how it relates to other works. If food and wine can be art, then they should exhibit similar cognitive demands. If, however, sensory enjoyment of wine or food does not require knowledge, they may lack the complexity and cognitive significance of a genuine art.

In the arts, knowledge of the techniques involved in artistic production, along with theories about art, enhance sensory experience. Knowing what artistic movements were in process at the time a work was created will make us more sensitive to certain features of the painting in comparison to earlier works. For example, the impressionists of the late nineteenth century were not concerned only with painting pretty pictures.

They were focused on how different atmospheric conditions modified the appearance of light. This complex interaction of light and atmosphere is easy to pass over in the absence of some understanding of what the impressionists thought they were doing. Similarly, our sensuous engagement with a building can be influenced by knowledge of its age, which makes us more aware of the depredations of time. By focusing on a building's age we experience how transitory grandeur is, how quickly brilliance can fade, and how age can mute rough edges or soften boundaries. Thus, knowledge of age directs our attention to texture and the beauty that arises from destruction.

Knowledge directs our attention to features we might otherwise miss. Through intimate knowledge of how a painting was created, we become acquainted with how color is mixed and applied and how different brush sizes cause different effects on the canvas. The smell, texture, and weight of the paint and the properties of the canvas gain their own resonance and remind us of the materiality of painting, a struggle to control physical materials that have their own recalcitrance. This knowledge of the process of painting not only guides our perceptions but also gives us an understanding of how an artist has worked with or against the opportunities and limitations made available by her materials and genre. Thus, through knowledge of process we acquire an affection for a work that influences our sensuous enjoyment of it.

In fact, the ability to have a sensory experience at all may depend on knowledge. To the uninitiated, the music of Arnold Schoenberg sounds like noise with no discernible pattern of musical composition. However, listeners who learn the logic of the twelve-tone row (the kind of musical scale employed by Schoenberg) and become practiced at discerning the complex musical patterns enabled by the abandonment of conventional harmonic structure are able to experience genuine sensuous beauty.

Thus, in the arts, there cannot be a sharp distinction between cognitive understanding and sensuous pleasure. They work together to enable appreciation. Knowledge aids appreciation through directing our attention to relevant aesthetic features, through creating feelings of affection for a work that enhance sensory experience, and by making us aware of patterns that otherwise might be unavailable to us. (I'm ignoring the sort of knowledge that is essential to understanding the meaning of a work of art, which I discuss in detail in the next chapter.)

Is there a comparable relationship between sensuous pleasure and knowledge with regard to wine or food? According to philosopher Kent Bach, the answer is no, at least with regard to wine. Regarding art appreciation, Bach writes:

> In the case of art and music, this is a very complex ability generally requiring at least some formal training and historical knowledge, including familiarity with other works and, in the case of music, other performances, to go along with perceptual acuity. Acquiring such knowledge leads to aesthetic appreciation by enhancing one's ability to notice features and relationships that would otherwise escape one's attention. No such knowledge is required for appreciating a wine. Even the best wines are not works of art. They don't have cognitive or emotional content. Their aesthetic value is provided entirely by the aromas and flavours that they impart. [17]

Thus, according to Bach, practice at discerning flavor and texture patterns may be necessary for appreciating wine, but knowledge of wine regions or winemaking processes are not necessary for sensuous enjoyment.

I've already argued that the emotional dimensions of food and wine are more extensive than Bach allows. He is equally mistaken about their cognitive dimension. If certain kinds of sensuous enjoyment are more readily available when we have relevant knowledge of the practice of art, I see no reason why knowledge of the practice of winemaking would not yield a similar sensuous engagement with wine. This argument holds for knowledge of how food is sourced and prepared as well. Knowledge of how grapes are grown, facts about the geography and weather conditions that influenced the grapes, and knowledge of winemaking practices can direct our attention to particular flavor profiles in wine in just the way knowledge of an artist's intentions or the age of a building focuses our attention on the relevant aesthetic features of paintings or buildings. The taste of a wine is a complex whole with many dimensions, some of which are obscured and partially hidden by dominant flavors. Wine knowledge helps unravel this complex whole and enables us to gain greater sensory awareness of its elements. The same can be said for foods if their flavors are sensitive to growing conditions or to cooking methods.

Are these sensory features unavailable in the absence of knowledge? Are we utterly unable to sense them without deep knowledge of production processes? I think the answer is probably no, but we are less likely to focus on them or be aware of their existence, and less likely to appreciate them in the absence of knowledge that makes production factors stand out as significant. I might be able to sense the difference between a mild vanilla flavor note and a rich coconut aroma in a Cabernet. But without knowing the significance of the decision to use French or American oak, I'm unlikely to pay attention to the difference in flavor. It is less likely to provoke attentional focus without the influence of knowledge.

Furthermore, knowledge of grape-growing and winemaking practices gives us a palpable awareness of the challenges of winemaking and the materiality of the process, and enables us to assess how well the wine-making operation performed given the challenges of climate and geography. If the materiality of paint yields a kind of affection that enhances our sensuous response to a painting, I see no reason why a similar affection for the material dimensions of wine would not enhance our sensuous response to the wine. In fact, we know that affection makes us perceive other humans as more beautiful; a similar enhancement to the sensory pleasures of wine would also seem a natural response.

Finally, although flavor notes and tactile impressions may be, in principle, individually discernible without substantial cognitive engagement, I doubt that a finely honed, discriminating sense of balance, structure, elegance, or finesse is likely without knowledge of what is in balance or what the elements of structure are. In fact, it is not obvious that the detection of balance, structure, elegance, and finesse are wholly sensory responses. Just as unity, symmetry, and balance in art require a grasp of how complex elements fit together as a whole, so do these notions when applied to wine. This holistic judgment, while in part sensory, would seem to require an intellectual grasp of relations, again indicating that a sharp distinction between intellectual and sensory pleasures is untenable.

In summary, just as in the appreciation of art, knowledge aids appreciation of wine and food through directing our attention to relevant aesthetic features, by creating feelings of affection for foods and beverages that enhance sensory experience, and by making us aware of patterns of flavors and aromas that we might otherwise pass over. The sensory and the cognitive are not distinct faculties but work together to create this sense of wonder that is at the heart of our fascination with food.

A PROMISE OF HAPPINESS

We have now strayed far from a basic model of food and wine providing only simple sensory pleasure. The pleasures of food and drink are complex interactions of sensory and cognitive capacities that I've referred to as yielding beauty. These references to beauty may strike some readers as quaint. If you have followed discussions of art by the art intelligentsia over the last century, you will find that beauty has been largely evacuated from the realm of art. But that has been a mistake; when we ignore beauty we ignore the ability of a work to attract, and thus begin to lose our grip on what motivates the enjoyment of art, which without beauty becomes an arid intellectual enterprise.

We find beauty in men and women, great works of art, nature, mathematical formulas, food and drink. What do these all have in common that make them beautiful? It won't be some set of fixed characteristics, for what counts as beauty changes with each beautiful object we encounter. The great novelist Stendhal wrote that beauty is the promise of happiness. I take it that he means it is not the works themselves that promise happiness but our relationship with them that produces that promise. Some works are tragic, sad, despairing—anything but happy. But our involvement with them may nevertheless enrich our lives.

To find something beautiful is not just to think it pretty, attractive, or good tasting. When we find something beautiful we feel there is something more to it that has not yet been discovered, our relationship with it has not exhausted its value, we want it to be repeated again and again. Great works of art, when we find them beautiful, haunt us even when they are not present, and we look forward to our next encounter as if it were a new experience. But even simple things—natural objects, a poet's word, a ceremony, a piece of furniture, things that resonate with the spirit of who made them—can have that aura of mystery and incompleteness about them. But since we don't know what has not yet been discovered, we cannot articulate precisely what that quality is that we find so compelling. This is the bane of all art criticism. We can speak about the beautiful, but the words are by necessity inadequate.

Food and wine can also have this quality of mystery and incompleteness that seem bound up with beauty. Of course, "tasting good" is not sufficient. Chocolate ice cream tastes good, but it's hard to conjure a sense of mystery about it. But food and wine that refer to the people who produce it, that have the mysterious ability to gather people and create community, that succeed in anchoring a sense of identity, that command us to take time to focus on the moment and recognize the intrinsic value of things, or that are starkly and utterly original—such edible things can be beautiful because they promise to make further contact with them worthwhile.

I'm inclined to think beauty (as opposed to the picturesque) is just that ineffable sense of mystery that some art objects have, the promise of something more that lies just beyond our comprehension that demands we explore it further—a form of transcendence. Philosopher Alexander Nehamas has turned Stendhal's comment into a robust theory of the beautiful. From Nehamas's perspective, when I find an object beautiful, I desire to have that object in my life and devote part of my life to it, and the object promises to make my life better when I become so committed. To find an object beautiful is to love it and to wish to care for it as well as discover its secrets.[18]

Beauty inspires commitment because it is an inexhaustible source of meaning—our love for the object resists settling on a final meaning, as Nehamas argues. We keep interpreting the beautiful object, compelled to discover why we love it, and to the extent we get no final answer the satisfaction of our desire is always just beyond our reach and there is no way of knowing where that desire will lead. If we were to settle on a final meaning, we would fall out of love with the object, having exhausted its potential. Immersed in changing, unpredictable desires, our lives then change in unpredictable ways leading us to "other people, other objects, other habits, and ways of being."[19] We are vulnerable to the object's call to us and we surrender to it. Thus, as we continue to surrender and long for satisfaction we engage with others, for through their insight we hope to find answers. As Nehamas writes, "The desire beauty provokes is essentially social: it literally does create a new society for it needs to be communicated to others and pursued in their company."[20] But the pursuit of beauty is fraught with peril. This is why beauty is "only a promise" of happiness. There are no guarantees that making something a part of your life will turn out well.

What about works of art that are disturbing or that deal with an ugly subject matter? Can they be beautiful and promise happiness? The violence of Picasso's *Guernica*, the desolate personalities of Kathe Kollwitz, the brutal angst of Munch's *The Scream*—all depictions of the horrible that we find fascinating or gripping. When painting, literature, or music expresses something unpleasant we don't experience it as unpleasant; we don't recoil from these works and run screaming from the museum in a fit of rage or fright. The spectacle of an artist relishing violence and mayhem is itself seductive and the contrast between the blindness of atrocity and the prurient insight we gain from viewing is part of the seduction—we take pleasure in the presentation. The depiction may be of something unpleasant, but through the artistry of the artist our experience is of something vivid, intense, and full of life. The actual experience of violence or trauma is deeply unpleasant, but its presentation via art nevertheless gives us pleasure. If this were not the case, we would feel repulsion rather than enchantment when confronted with great art. We are moved by great art, but it is always the pleasure we take in the representation that participates in our being moved. Art that gives no pleasure is simply a failed work.

Some commentators have argued that food cannot be art because it is incapable of representing the ugly. Food (and wine) has to taste good. Otherwise we won't consume it no matter how interesting it is. We take food into our bodies, so we are very careful to avoid anything that might be dangerous or disgusting. Thus some have concluded that food lacks the expressive range of painting, music, or literature because, whatever food does, it must do so with pleasure. But fine art and fine food and wine do not differ in the role that pleasure plays in the experience—it is necessary for both and in both cases that pleasure is an indicator of beauty.

Moreover, it is simply false that food does not represent violence or horror. The carcass of a dead fish with one eye staring at you is unlovely and it represents a variety of ideas—death, slaughter, power, and the creative destruction of heat among others. It is the artistry of the chef and our own powers of self-deception that cast that violence in the glow of phenomenological pleasure. There is nothing in ordinary life more violent than the act of eating. We rend and tear at our food after it has been slaughtered, butchered, and burned to a crisp—and then we swallow and assimilate it to our own substance. Yet we are attracted to the act of eating via the pangs of hunger and the charms of flavor and aroma. All eating represents the horrible and the grotesque. That we fail to attend to it is testimony both to our capacity for self-deception and the talents of chefs who induce us to find pleasure in their presentation.

The presence of beauty is always apparent in the appearance of the object and the pleasure we take in it, but the reasons for me finding something beautiful can never be fully articulated because there are no rules for beauty and each instance of it is unique. No object fully shares its aesthetic properties with any other object. To experience beauty in something is to see what belongs to it uniquely, and that in turn is to see it in a way that is distinctly "our own." The recognition of beauty is thus not the mere identification of a quality that some object possesses; the recognition of beauty is intrinsically motivational. We don't passively look at beautiful objects but are instead drawn to them—they move us, invite our engagement because the recognition of beauty is a form of love. We cannot help but love what we find beautiful and find beautiful what we love, according to Nehamas. [21]

The examples of art to which Nehamas refers in order to illustrate his claims about beauty are primarily from the visual arts. But contemporary foodies and their fellow aficionados in the world of beverages fit Nehamas's conception of seekers after beauty, for it is very much about making food part of your life. The foodie who tracks down the origin of her lamb chops and the wine lover who seeks to penetrate the mysteries of *terroir* have indeed fallen in love.

Thus, what begins with pleasure takes on a larger assemblage of meanings. Culinarians do not simply taste, feel a rush of pleasure, and then run off to the next experience. Taste becomes a practice, a discipline, an intellectual challenge for which the payoff is in part intellectual. The world of food and beverage, among those committed to its geography and structure, is not by and large a world constituted entirely by a desire for virtuoso performances and stunning effects, the excesses of TV food shows notwithstanding. It is a world in which knowledge and understanding matter, a world in which the characteristically human practice of creating meaning is its reason to exist. It is time now to explore how food and beverage become meaningful.

5

HOW TO READ A MEAL
The Flavor of Symbols

You will encounter it when surrounded by the shimmering symphony of blues, greens, and lavenders in Monet's water lilies, or when transfixed by the soft, supple, yet steel-edged voice of Billie Holiday, or even when you find a quiet garden to while away an afternoon. Sometimes you even find it in a luxurious beef bourguignon. Beauty's calling card, the sheer sensual delight in the appearances of things, attracts us to art in the first place before any thought of "profundity" or "insight."

Like art, food and wine give us plenty of sensual delight. As explained in the previous chapter, sensual delight can provoke emotions, making food and wine an expressive medium, and it stimulates reflection on the nature of our experience securing a contemplative, analytical dimension for food and wine as robust as that of music or the visual arts. However, there is more to this contemplative, analytical dimension than I have discussed thus far. Works of art do not merely give us sensuous experiences to contemplate; they are rich with meanings, they are about something and demand that we interpret them. Human beings are the "meaning giving" animal and cannot let appearances be. We demand of art that it tell us about ourselves and our world. Can we make the same demands of food and wine?

This demand that meaning should trump sensual pleasure is an assumption that lurks behind much art criticism. Although acknowledging its importance, most art criticism quickly moves beyond sensuality to a search for profound meaning—that an object provides sensual pleasure is not enough to certify it as great art. This strain of debilitating asceticism is a holdover from the modernist movements in the twentieth century, discussed briefly in the previous chapter, which cultivated an anti-aesthetic sensibility. For the avant-garde, the pursuit of beauty was a trivial aim not worthy of great art. Art should change things, shock and unsettle us. It should awaken people from conformity and convention and confront them with the real world and the possibility of changing it. Art is about ideas or powerful emotional reactions to suffering, not the apprehension of good taste.

Even works by great masters are criticized when they seem to lack profound insight. The nineteenth-century French artist Pierre-August Renoir produced works of great visual appeal and technical sophistication, but many of his paintings are criticized for excessive sentimentality, depicting a shallow conception of life that overlooks its darker side. Works such as Warhol's *Brillo Boxes* and Duchamp's *Fountain* did much to move aesthetics off the agenda. The "look" of Warhol's *Brillo Boxes* in a gallery is nearly identical to the "look" of Brillo boxes on the store shelf. Yet one is art and the other not. So it cannot be visual appearance that makes an object a work of art. And when artists and critics take seriously an upside-down urinal as an art object, as they did when Marcel Duchamp's *Fountain* was displayed in 1917, clearly visual appearance no longer matters, unless one is a connoisseur of urinals. What matters are the ideas that such interventions express.

However, you don't have to endorse this anti-aesthetic attitude to grasp the importance of meaning in art. It would be absurd to claim that what is most interesting about Hieronymus Bosch's *The Garden of Earthly Delights* is the visual appearance instead of the meaning of the characters cavorting around this cauldron of licentious activity. The swirling brush strokes and striking colors of Munch's *The Scream* are stunning but not more important than the fact that the painting seems to represent a painful form of alienation and loneliness. In fact, the visual look gives the impression of alienation. The visual appeal of the surface works together with the content of a work—that is, what the work is about—to produce meaning.

Even abstract art has meaning. Work that doesn't appear to be about an object at all can sometimes express and provoke powerful feelings and ideas. The chaotic and fragmented splashes of color in Wassily Kandinsky's *Ravine Improvisation* don't appear to represent anything. But Kandinsky claimed they were expressions of color as a boundless, immeasurable quality that constitutes a brief for spirituality against the cold, measurable rationalism of science and technology. To Mark Rothko, his intensely beautiful blocks of layered color conveyed a sense of isolation, hopelessness, and doubt, and they do give the viewer a sense of floating in a limitless color-world without mooring or anchor.

As consummate meaning-mongers, humans can supply meaning to almost anything if we work at it. Of course, one might accuse Kandinsky and Rothko of manufacturing meanings to alleviate the worry that they are merely making pretty pictures. But the very fact that artists, their critics, and the public strive to infuse these works with meaning suggests that the attribution of meaning is simply non-optional however remote or implausible. Because "meaning-mongering" is a staple of contemporary art criticism, edible arts must also have meaning if they are to occupy their rightful place as fine art, although ideally their meaning will not be as factitious as the meaning some critics attach to abstract art.

But can food really tell us about ourselves or the world? Here is a quote from essayist and literary critic William Deresiewic articulating the standard puzzlement often expressed when confronted by this question of the meaning of food:

> But food, for all that, is not art. Both begin by addressing the senses, but that is where food stops. It is not narrative or representational, does not organize and express emotion. An apple is not a story, even if we can tell a story about it. A curry is not an idea, even if its creation is the result of one. Meals can evoke emotions, but only very roughly and generally, and only within a very limited range—comfort, delight, perhaps nostalgia, but not anger, say, or sorrow, or a thousand other things. Food is highly developed as a system of sensations, extremely crude as a system of symbols. Proust on the madeleine is art; the madeleine itself is not art. A good risotto is a fine thing, but it isn't going to give you insight into other people, allow you to see the world in a new way, or force you to take an inventory of your soul.[1]

I dealt with the claim that food cannot express emotion in the previous chapter. In this chapter and the next I will focus on meaning. I will argue that critiques like that of Deresiewic are mistaken; food does provide us with a meaningful system of symbols sufficient to qualify at least some food as works of art. However, the dismissive argument from Deresiewic receives support from many philosophers throughout history writing on the arts. Many of these arguments have been soundly refuted in recent years as food and wine have received a bit more philosophical attention. Claims that tastes are too subjective, too transitory, or too functional stumble badly when held up to scrutiny, largely because many of the other media we consider art are transitory, functional, and provoke subjective responses as well. However, skeptical questions persist about whether food preparations have the right kind of meaning to be treated as fine art. Even Carolyn Korsmeyer, the philosopher most responsible for putting food on the philosophical map, while granting that food is worthy of serious attention, has reservations about food being a fine art: "Ought we now to take the next step and conclude that foods also qualify as works of art in the full sense of the term? That they represent in their own medium the same sorts of objects as paintings, sculptures, poems, and symphonies? I do not believe we should."[2]

Korsmeyer's objection to food as art is based on reasons to think food acquires meaning differently than the objects of visual or auditory experience. Food, she argues, acquires meaning because of its context, the ceremonies and rituals that surround the serving of food; the objects represented by paintings or symphonies are less dependent on context. When we consider food aesthetically and pay attention to how food tastes we risk ignoring those contextual factors that give food its meaning; by contrast when we consider paintings or music aesthetically we gain greater access to their meaning. Thus, there are asymmetries in the comparison of food and art that disqualify food from consideration as fine art.

To answer such skepticism it would be useful to consider how paintings acquire meaning. What is the difference between a pretty picture and a work of visual art? Works of art are about something—the starry skies, a girl with a pearl earring, the ravages of time—and thus demand interpretation. They ask us to ponder what they mean. By contrast, pretty pictures are just pretty and make few interpretive demands on us. Works of art provoke us to pay attention to their subject matter. They provide a uniquely powerful mode of access to the world depicted in the painting and give us a new way of seeing it.

By contrast, food does not appear to represent an independent object in the way the *Mona Lisa* represents a woman with an enigmatic smile. We do not see ourselves or the world in light of a "food depiction." Food flavors and textures may be interesting, but their arrangement lacks the rich cluster of references to something beyond themselves that works of visual art have, according to this critique. Does it make sense to speak of interpretation when eating a tuna casserole, even if it were deconstructed and gussied up with parmesan foam and spherical olives? Apparently there are sharp differences between art and food that render talk of "culinary art" at best pretentious and at worst incoherent. If the edible arts are to be taken seriously as genuine fine arts rather than crafts or "applied art," they must supply us with more than flavor experiences, regardless of how varied, intense, or provocative. They must supply meaning, but they do so in only very limited ways, or so the skeptic argues.

Of course, in one trivial sense, food can depict events and objects in much the same way a painting does. Food can be made to resemble objects just as a portrait resembles the model who sits for it. For example, the croissant is shaped like a crescent and, according to one legend, was invented by the Viennese to celebrate the defeat of the Ottomans who, with crescents on their flags, had laid siege to the city. Pretzels do a good job of depicting how my students think; perhaps a pretzel accompanying a low score on an exam might make their failure more salient to them. But beyond the occasional stunt or oddity, food is limited as a medium for visual depiction. If food is an art, it cannot be because of its capacity for visual representation.

This claim that food lacks meaning will provoke howls of protest from the increasing hordes of food fanatics willing to hire a guide and a yak to find the best mo-mo in the Himalayas. Eating is not just eating but also a form of communication, they insist. The anthropologists and sociologists who study foodways agree. Don't food preferences express cultural identities, symbolize our origins and allegiances, and signal to others our commitment to various values such as sustainability or authenticity? Of course, the answer is yes. Food is richly symbolic. The apple in Eve's hand represents the fall of humanity. The apple in Mom's apple pie represents her loving solicitude. The apple in the tree signifies the arrival of autumn. For the Genoan, the taste of home is pesto; for coastal New Englanders, it's a clambake. Chicken soup is a symbol of healing; the Thanksgiving turkey a symbol of gratitude, abundance, and the gathering of family. There is plenty of meaning here to keep the semioticians busy. The same can be said about wines if they have a strong connection to place.

The skeptics do not deny the symbolic significance of food but will distinguish two kinds of symbols, only one of which is characteristic of fine art. When food has meaning, they claim, the context in which food is produced and consumed supplies the meaning, not the features of the food itself. There is a narrative that makes Eve's apple a symbol of the fall of humanity. Without the biblical story, the apple is just a piece of fruit. There is a habit of association and a story about Thanksgiving Day that makes turkey a symbol of gratitude. Without the narrative and the habit of association, the turkey is just a cooked bird. There is nothing about turkeys, on their own, that demands interpretation unless there is a surrounding narrative to make the demand. After all, a slab of dull, desiccated meat slathered with salty, flour-stiffened soup stock doesn't scream gratitude. It's the thought that counts. The same is true of the contribution of food to cultural and moral identities. To the Genoan, pesto is meaningful because it comes from Genoa, not because of its flavors or textures, however much they may be appreciated. When apple pie brings tender memories of hearth and home to mind, it is personal association carrying the load, not the intrinsic meaning of the flavor of apples.

The skeptic will further insist that food and wine fail to be the source of new insight. Certain foods may remind us of home or reinforce cultural identities, but the flavors themselves do not provide us with new discoveries about anything except flavors; they tell us little about ourselves or our world unless we gin up a narrative to give them interpretive significance. To be clear, the skeptic is not claiming we are never gobsmacked by the experience of a meal or wine that plumbs the depths of our being, only that such gobsmacking is not sufficient to qualify an object as a work of art, since it relies too much on personal context rather than intrinsic meaning.

This is not how meaning develops in works of art. Edvard Munch's *The Scream* is a good example of how features internal to a painting produce meaning. *The Scream* is a symbol of alienation because of the aesthetic properties of the painting. The skull-like shape of the head, the featureless face that focuses attention on the mouth, and the position of the body in relation to the other people on the bridge indicate alienation; the swirling, lurid colors express intense negative emotion. These meanings are in the painting, not in an external narrative or context. Granted, even for a painting such as *The Scream*, context is important for a comprehensive interpretation. It helps to know that Munch intended that the painting express alienation and that he was painting at a time when modern humanity was confronting an industrial age that ripped people from their traditional moorings. Nevertheless, much of the meaning of the painting is carried by features of the painting itself, not the surrounding narrative. If you the viewer have had a powerful experience of personal estrangement, the painting may have intense emotional resonance. However, despite these contextual factors, the internal features of the painting give us primary access to the meaning of the work, not the cultural or psychological contexts. Those intrinsic features provoke the powerful response we have toward the painting, and that intrinsic meaning is the essence of fine art. Thus, the thesis that food can be art must confront the objection that food, even when finely prepared and creatively conceived, lacks intrinsic meaning. The flavors and textures are not about anything unless we supply some story, ritual, ceremony, or personal association that makes them be about something. But then the task of generating meaning is not performed by the work (the dish or meal) but by the cultural narratives that surround it. Wine suffers the same fate—its meaning is generated by how it is used or where it is from, not by its flavors and textures.

A mealy apple still brings to mind the fall of humanity. It performs its symbolic function even if it is not very tasty. A dry and under-seasoned Turkey is still a celebration of Thanksgiving despite its failure as an aesthetic object. This is not so in the case of *The Scream*. The power of its representation of alienation depends crucially on the vividness of the color and the formal arrangement of the figures in the painting. This is the heart of the argument that food cannot be a genuine work of fine art. The psychological and social context is supplying the meaning, not the flavors and texture themselves. As insightful as the modernist chefs have been in writing about the art of gastronomy, they don't directly confront this issue, which is at the core of philosophical objections to food as art.

I think this argument denying intrinsic meaning to food (and wine) is wrongheaded. Food and wine have a variety of meanings that are central to our lives, and these meanings are generated by the flavors and textures, the aesthetic properties, themselves. Thus, my focus in what follows is to show that the symbolic function of food—its ability to stand for the home, family traditions, cultural identities, romance—in part depends on flavor, texture, on how the food tastes. In this respect it is no different from the way visual art acquires meaning.

THE FLAVORS OF HOME

When we eat, if we pay attention at all, we focus on the pleasures of flavor and texture. But some meals have a larger significance that provokes memory and imagination. So it is with comfort food—the filling, uncomplicated, soft, and digestible comestibles that haunt our consciousness with thoughts of security, calm, nourishment, and being cared for, especially when triggered by memories of the flavors of home. Apple pie, ice cream, chocolate cake, macaroni and cheese, chicken soup—their smell and taste can unfetter a flood of memories because our brains are wired to associate good feelings with specific flavors and aromas, especially when the flavors are fat, salt, and sugar. In the face of such powerful stimuli, we succumb helplessly to the endorphin cascade.

The foods of home have such a grip on us that we go to a great deal of trouble to bring our food with us when we travel. The spread of various foodstuffs throughout the world was made possible by armies, both military and migrant, determined to carry the taste of home with them. A visit to any "ethnic" market in a major city reveals the importance of these taste memories to our sense of well-being.

Home cooking has this significance because meals are as much about relationships as they are about food. Unlike other animals, we do not eat when food is available. We dine at particular times, in particular ways, and with particular tablemates. Families interact around the kitchen table and are defined by the small daily rituals of gathering, preparing, and consuming food. Meals bring families together physically and emotionally and the tastes and smells become associated with solace and acceptance.

"Homeyness," for want of a more elegant word, may be the most powerful and persistent meaning that attaches to food. Thus, the simplistic claim that food lacks meaning is obviously false. Mom's apple pie is as meaningful as anything in life for some of us. But does comfort food have the kind of meaning that works of art have? Do specific comfort foods represent home in the same sense that the *Mona Lisa* represents a woman with an enigmatic smile?

As I indicated above, many thinkers insist that meanings associated with food are quite different from meanings associated with art. According to this skeptical argument, Mom's apple pie means "homeyness" because it was made by Mom, with love and care, and it was eaten on many occasions when the family was together, bonds were reinforced, and family rituals enacted. But these family bonds are facts external to the pie. They give Mom's apple pie meaning, but they are not "in the pie" in the way that flavor and texture are "in the pie." The taste of the pie doesn't generate meaning according to this argument; the story of one's family and home life, the context, confers the meaning. Without knowing the context, one could not "read off" the pie, the meanings relevant to home and family. The pie has significance because it was served at home, not because there is something meaningful about its taste and smell. So the aesthetic properties of the pie are irrelevant to its meaning as comfort food.

This skeptical argument is right about some cases. I once had a Hawaiian acquaintance who professed a love for poi—the Hawaiian staple made from fermented taro root that gives the taste of library paste a bad name—because it reminded him so powerfully of home. In principle, any flavor profile, regardless of how bland or off-putting, could trigger thoughts of home if associated with the people and rituals of one's home, which suggests that flavor is not essential to meaning. But this is not always the case, and I doubt that it is typically the case. I will use my own experience as an example. While I recognize that an anecdote is not data, my aim is not so much to prove my point but to encourage readers to think about whether their experience resonates with mine.

In my home, the dish that has always signified "homeyness" is macaroni and cheese made from a recipe originally gleaned from an old Fanny Farmer cookbook, although I have modified and refined it over many years. This is not a special occasion dish; no charged emotional episodes heighten its significance. It is just a supper dish. Yet, when it is on the menu, it is met with much anticipation, consumed with glee, and followed with much remonstration about whether I got it right this time. I have it on good authority—namely, my wife and son—that the meaning of this dish is utterly dependent on its aesthetic properties. The precise flavor and texture characteristics explain why this dish has acquired its symbolic significance for us. But aside from this expert testimony, there is good evidence that it is flavor and texture that matter. Many other dishes I have made under similar circumstances do not acquire this significance, and I have made other versions of macaroni and cheese, with different flavor and texture characteristics, that are met with much less enthusiasm. There is something particular to this flavor and texture profile that explains its "homeyness." Apparently the aesthetic properties—flavor and texture—are generating meaning, despite the skepticism articulated above.

How do these flavors and textures stand as a symbol for the home? As I noted above, there are generic features of comfort food that conventionally signify comfort. The macaroni is soft and, with the cheese, forms a homogeneous mass which indicates security because there is nothing fussy, challenging, or complicated about it. The fat, protein, and bulky carbs are stick-to-the-ribs filling, indicating nourishment, and the fat and saltiness of the cheese give plenty of stimulation to the pleasure centers of the brain. The addition of apple, an unusual ingredient in macaroni and cheese, contributes sweetness, which conventionally signifies "the good life." These qualities tend to mean "comfort food," which has obvious connotations to the home. They are conventional symbols much like a dove that represents peace or a star that represents hope in a painting. But they also "highlight" comfort—the food possesses comforting characteristics that enable it to symbolize the comforts of home.

The flavor and texture profile of this dish came together over many years and is the result of an intention to satisfy the tastes of my family. Importantly, the care with which a dish is conceived and executed is indicated by the aesthetic features internal to the dish—especially the precision of the execution and the balance of flavors and textures. These features can be tasted. Yet they are not merely flavors—they have meaning because they lend themselves to interpretation. They mean "homeyness" because they highlight or exemplify the care and attention characteristic of home cooks.

Of course, precision of execution and fineness of conception do not always indicate the kind of care associated with the home. A well-trained restaurant chef can conceive and execute a dish while being utterly indifferent to diners. But in the context of home cooking, with limited time, money, and other factors placing constraints on a commitment to cooking, fineness of conception and precision of execution are plausibly interpreted as signifying a commitment to the quality of home life. Love and care are not "in the dish" in the way flavor and texture are "in the dish." But they are contextual features that help interpret precision of execution and fineness of conception, which are in the dish, as indicators of the love and care associated with the home. Thus, precision of execution and fineness of conception are symbols of love and care in this context. That one needs the appropriate background and history of experience to interpret the dish as such does not distinguish it from art. All interpretation requires the appropriate background and experience.

The third, and perhaps most important, reason for thinking the flavor and texture profile of this dish means "homeyness" is that it represents a shared sensibility. All members of my immediate family find this particular dish extraordinarily satisfying. The dish not only refers to this shared sensibility but also exemplifies it, represents it, and highlights it. The flavors display our shared sensibility just as the swirling brush strokes and juxtapositions of characters in *The Scream* both indicate alienation and demonstrate it.

This notion of a shared sensibility is important enough to dwell on for a moment. María Lugones, in her widely reprinted essay "Playfulness, 'World'-Traveling, and Loving Perception," writes that there are four ways of being at ease in a "world."[3] You can be at ease in a "world" because you are a fluent speaker of the language or agree with the norms that operate in that "world." In addition, you can be at ease in a "world" if you are bonded by love to other members of that "world" or share a history with them. But in her account of why she is incapable of being playful in certain "worlds" she enters, she leaves out an important dimension of being at ease or "at home." That dimension is a shared sensibility, shared "at easeness" with the physicality of what surrounds us.

Nothing indicates "homeyness" more than the familiarity of surfaces—the precise way the wind nips at the collar while doing chores in the late afternoon or the hand traces the contours of a porch railing, the wisdom of feet navigating without inhibition through a darkened basement, or perhaps most saliently the taste and smells of a familiar kitchen. Comfort food operates as a kind of synecdoche symbolizing the fullness of familiar sensations that constitute our dwelling in a particular place and with the people with whom we share a life. It is particular flavors and textures that stand for this sensibility. But they don't merely "stand for" it; they exemplify it. They show (via taste) what they mean.

But this is precisely what (some) art does. It puts us in touch with the elements of sensation, makes us aware of how these elements can be distinguished, separated, combined, and recombined to form the imaginative worlds that we inhabit. The home is one small part of that larger world to which artists are drawn to explore. But it is a part that is of a distinctly human scale that the edible arts are perhaps uniquely well equipped to explore.

I don't mean to suggest that all comfort foods that signify "homey-ness" are works of art—the goals of the home cook are typically different from those of an artistic chef. But this argument does suggest that some of the meanings that attach to food are the kind of meaning we associate with art, and that the differences between edible arts and fine arts are practical, not theoretical.

ROMANCE: A TISSUE OF LITTLE THINGS REVISITED

The ability of food to symbolize romance has become a cliché, especially around Valentine's Day when even the most desultory couple manages to build a castle with a box of chocolate. But the connection is in fact more profound than a once-a-year phantasm. In fact this symbolic connection is deeply rooted in history and seems virtually universal. Perhaps the most vivid demonstration of the symbolic link between food and romantic emotion is Laura Esquivel's novel (and subsequent film), *Like Water for Chocolate*. In this magical realist tale of a turn-of-the-twentieth-century Mexican family, Tita, the youngest daughter, communicates her emotions to her family through the food she makes for them. As she prepares the food, passion, longing, anger, or frustration are transmitted via the food to the people who eat the dish, who then experience similar emotions. When Tita falls in love with Pedro, the quail in rose petal sauce she serves at a family celebration induces lustful feelings in her sister Gertrudis, who abruptly leaves the ranch while making love to a soldier on the back of a horse. When Tita's older sister, Rosaura, marries Pedro, Tita sorrowfully prepares a wedding cake, which throws her guests into paroxysms of longing and melancholy before they become violently ill.

Of course, this novel is pure fantasy, but the idea that food directly stirs our emotions has a long history. The ancient Greeks, Egyptians, and Romans all entertained folk wisdom that various foods could induce sexual arousal, and the medical science and philosophy of the day was used to support such beliefs. We get the word "aphrodisiac" from Aphrodite, the Greek goddess of romantic love. According to the myth, Aphrodite was born from the sea and came to shore on a scallop shell accompanied by Eros, thus giving birth to the idea that shellfish can arouse sexual desire in lovers. Aphrodite also thought sparrows were particularly lust-ful. Thus, Europeans for many centuries considered sparrows an aphrodisiac, which shows that it doesn't take much to persuade people when the promise of sex is involved.

Oysters were a necessary part of any respectable Roman orgy, a practice perhaps influenced by the famous Roman physician Galen, who prescribed oysters to remedy a declining sexual appetite. Galen believed that any warm, moist food would be stimulating—as long as it produced flatulence. Galen's grasp of the idea of romance must surely be questioned, but his view was widely held until the eighteenth century, and foods such as asparagus, mustard, anise, and peas were considered aphrodisiacs for centuries because of Galen's influence. Even a thinker as staid and sober as St. Thomas Aquinas insisted that meat and wine would stimulate the libido. The concept of an aphrodisiac is not limited to Western culture. Bird's nest soup, sea cucumbers, and a variety of herbs and spices such as ginger, cloves, and ginseng have been commonly believed to be aphrodisiacs for centuries in various Asian cultures.

Of course, there is little scientific evidence of a causal effect between food and sexual arousal. Contemporary science shows that, at best, chocolate contains chemicals that can elevate mood, although a recent study has shown that a person weighing one hundred thirty pounds would have to consume twenty-five pounds of chocolate to have a significant effect. Chili peppers quicken the pulse and induce sweating, but that is hardly equivalent to romance.

Since there is little evidence of a causal connection between food and libido, stories such as *Like Water for Chocolate* are best viewed as demonstrating the power of food as a symbol or metaphor for romance. If food is to be a metaphor for romance, there must be sufficient similarities between them to make the connection stick. In what ways are food and romance similar? They both serve functions deeply rooted in our biological needs. Human beings need food to continue living and sex to perpetuate the species, and both are required to satisfy bodily urges. It is therefore not surprising that throughout history people have used food as a metaphoric symbol of romance in ceremonies such as the marriage feast.

The concept of a marriage feast is ubiquitous, seemingly present in every region of the world throughout history. Generations of anthropologists have been fascinated by the marriage rituals of Papua New Guinea, in which the families of the bride and groom stage an elaborate eight-step process of exchanging food gifts that must be completed before the wedding can take place. Mesopotamian stone tablets from four thousand years ago tell us that a wedding was concluded by anointing the head of a bride with oil and organizing a banquet in her honor. The symbolic connection between food and procreation was well established in ancient Rome, where cake was thrown at the bride because the Romans believed its main ingredients, wheat and barley, were symbols of fertility. The American custom of throwing rice at newlyweds has the same origin. In parts of rural China, newlyweds find their matrimonial bed strewn with candied lotus seeds because the lotus is a prolific seed producer, and when cooked with lentils they symbolize the traditional hope that the newlyweds will be blessed with many children. Food as a symbol of romance travels well. It is easy to see why so many disparate peoples have made this connection—romance signals fertility, among many other meanings, and our ability to procreate depends on the fertility of the plants and animals that we eat. Food is the product of the generative capacities of plants and animals and is thus a natural symbol of the generative capacities of human beings. The connotations of fertility can be easily transferred from one semantic domain to the other.

These associations between food and fertility depend on the similarities of the functions of each. But what about the intrinsic properties of food—flavors and textures and the pleasure they produce? Are there similarities between the pleasures associated with food and the pleasures associated with romance that reinforce the idea that food is a symbol of romance? Our language suggests so. Most of the words we use to describe our positive, aesthetic reactions to food—delicious, mouthwatering, scrumptious, savory, sweet, luscious, delectable, appetizing, and so forth—are used to metaphorically describe a romantic partner. In both food and sex, pleasure is derived from tactile sensations. Chilis light up the senses (if they don't burn too much). The appeal of chocolate is largely tactile, gaining its sensuous edge from its mouth caressing viscosity, which enables it to also symbolize luxury, decadence, and indulgence, all of which have connections with romance. (The preparation of food is highly tactile as well, although pounding, cutting, kneading, and tearing are hopefully not associated with romance.) The flavors of some foods produce meanings that are sometimes associated with romance. Vanilla is soothing and comforting. Peppermint has an uplifting effect that may have to do as much with mouthfeel as it does with flavor. Sugar and sweet foods, throughout much of human history, have represented the good life, the rich life, or the full life. Romance is a central part of lives so described.

Soup picks up another dimension of romance. It connotes feelings of belonging, well-being, and warmth, and it is a means of self-fortification and restoration as well, benefits that soup shares with romance. But this is in part because most soup is served warm and is soft, mouth-coating, and easy to consume, with evocative, familiar aromas. Perhaps more important, the idea of hunger applies to both food and romance. Both "hungers" are among the most powerful and fundamental expressions of human need, and it is with this shared meaning that food maintains its most poignant reference to the domain of the erotic. But, once again, that hunger is often a craving for specific flavors just as the hunger of romance is for a specific person. It is not some narrative about food but the food itself that we crave.

The relationship of alcohol to romance is perhaps even more direct. Alcohol causes exhilaration and relaxation and is often used to enhance mood, thus symbolizing the allure and charm of romance. But it also signals (because it directly causes) physical and emotional release, thus paralleling the dimensions of romance that involve "falling," "letting go," or "giving in." However, the relationship between the pleasures of food and the pleasures of romance goes beyond mere resemblance. Food exemplifies or highlights romantic sensuality in much the same way that music, of the right sort, exemplifies it. The trajectory of romance—the anticipation, heightened arousal, and gratification—is often captured by the way music flows, mimicking the movement of the various emotions that grace a romantic evening. Approached with the proper attention, food can exhibit a similar structure, captured well by food writer Jennifer Ianollo's evocative prose:

> To elevate eating to a form of art is to turn all of existence into a radiant canvas, where all that is wonderful in nature can be embraced in one sitting, as our eyes and nose take in the first hints of the pleasures to come. Our salivary glands respond, eager to take the first bite. As the texture of that bite coats our palate, we are engulfed with fragrance and hints of sweet or savory, then the full rhapsody of flavor and its after taste.[4]

Although contemporary references to "foodgasms" may be a bit hyperbolic, feelings of being enveloped in a moment of pure beauty are characteristic of food, as well as romance and music. But of course that feeling of being enveloped in a moment of beauty depends crucially on the flavors and textures of the food, which highlight and thus symbolize the feeling of being engulfed by the presence of the beloved.

But to experience the most profound form of enjoyment that both food and romance have to offer, we have to look beyond the more superficial kinds of sensual gratifications to which I have been alluding thus far. Romance connects us to something larger than ourselves—a relationship that becomes more than the sum of the individuals that make it up, the beginnings of a community, a way of seeing the world through someone else's eyes. It is an activity in which one must give as well as take and thus involves self-knowledge, knowledge of the beloved—thought. Part of the enjoyment of romance is an intellectual apprehension.

As described in chapter 1, it was Rousseau who said that "taste is knowing the tissue of little things that make up the agreeableness of life." The ability of food to exemplify romance is based on the fact that both food and romance involve sharing the "tissue of little things," the everyday moments of satisfaction that make up the real substance of a life. Of all our personal belongings, it is food we most readily share with others. That sharing involves an investment of time and energy, and the full enjoyment of both romantic relationships and food requires sustained commitment. The desire to nourish and satisfy others is at the center of both romance and food preparation. Both express care because they exemplify care—and, as I argued in chapter 3, flavor and texture are essential to the expressiveness of food. Thus, both food and romance share a *telos*—an end—that enable one to stand for the other.

YOU ARE WHAT YOU EAT

Food also functions as a symbol of who we are, a flag we can wave when identity is threatened. Of course, human beings fight about a lot of things. But food fights play a special role in our fisticuff economy—they fill the time when we are between wars. Beans or meat alone in a proper chili? Fish or fowl in a proper paella? Vegetarians against meat eaters. Locavores against factory farmers. Questions like these divide nations, regions, and families. Taboos against eating certain foods have always been a way of marking off a zone of conflict. Kosher and halal rules have little justification aside from the symbolic power of defining one's perceived enemy as engaging in what is forbidden by expressing disgust at what the Other eats.

Conflict persists even when food is intended as entertainment. The competition for global culinary capo continues to heat up. The French jealously guarded their supremacy for centuries until supplanted by the upstart Spanish with their molecular concoctions, only to be cast out by the Norwegians, who have convinced us of the savor of weeds. Meanwhile the Italians wait for the fennel dust to settle, confident that in the end we always return to pasta and pizza.

The dishes we consume or refuse express our style, our values, and the allegiances to which we pledge. And so it has always been. "Tell me what you eat: I will tell you what you are," wrote Brillat-Savarin in 1825. Beyond flavor, food apparently has a "moral taste" as well. It figures in our self-image, in who we think we are, as individuals, as members of a community, as a nation. And this "moral taste" is no inconsequential preference or liking. It matters and matters deeply. The vegetarian not only prefers vegetables and sees herself as a vegetarian but also is taking a moral stance—she or he takes pride in the stance, sees it as a project, a commitment superior in value to the alternatives. The Italian feels the same about eating Italian. It means slow eating, communal eating, *la dolce vita*. A taste for pesto is not merely a preference for the combination of garlic, olive oil, basil, and Parmigiano Reggiano. It is a moral taste that carries meaning. Contemporary gastrophiles exhibit the same kind of zealous commitment. The search for the best barbecue in town is not just a search for a good meal but also a quest for a peak experience, a realization of a standard, a moral commitment to refuse the taste of the ordinary. Food is thus deeply bound up with our identities as members of the social groups to which we belong.

It is easy to see why food serves as an anchor for moral identity. We take food into our bodies. It is the source of our energy, a persistent pursuit, the focal point of family life. It hits us where we live. To quote Brillat-Savarin again, "The pleasures of the table are for every man, of every land, and no matter of what place in history or society; they can be a part of all his other pleasures, and they last the longest, to console him when he has outlived the rest." But how important is "mouth taste" to "moral taste." Do particular flavors matter in determining what we commit to and what we reject? After all, it is Italy the Italians love (or, more precisely, the region of Italy from which they hail). That basil, olive oil, garlic, and Parmigiano Reggiano happen to be indigenous to Genoa is just an accident of history. If those flavors did not exist, some other flavor profile would serve just as well to anchor Genoan identity. Similarly, the moral commitment to vegetarianism is what matters to the vegetarian. The preference for vegetables follows behind, a habit made necessary by that commitment, a dessert to the main moral meal. Ideology trumps taste, or so it would seem.

This is certainly how many social scientists view matters. Food preferences are markers of identity or signs of social status, a kind of fashion statement that signals to others our commitment to certain values. Eating is not just eating but also a form of communication. It's about moral taste; mouth taste is a source of subjective enjoyment but carries no larger significance. To the anthropologist, sociologist, or economist, fine cuisine is about class distinction, French cuisine about national distinction, food taboos about contrasts with the other, and so forth. The pleasure of food is just an empty cipher in a game of divide and conquer, all accompanied by an assumption that one's own way of eating is the right way.

But a significant explanatory hurdle confronts this way of looking at things. Tastes change very rapidly in the modern world, and transform our moral identities. Whatever role these "moral tastes" play, they don't appear to supply "mouth tastes" with fixed meanings. For example, what precisely is a vegetarian? Technically, a vegetarian eats no meat. But in reality, matters are more complicated. There are lacto-vegetarians, ovo-vegetarians, or lacto-ovo-vegetarians who eat no meat but will eat milk and/or eggs. Some vegetarians will eat fish or seafood but avoid all other meat, but many people are semi-vegetarians eating dairy products and eggs as well as some chicken and fish but no red meat. Dietary vegans do not eat animals or animal derivatives but may use animals in other commodities. But ethical vegans refuse to use any animal product, including dairy products, eggs, honey, wool, leather, and cosmetics, and in some cases they avoid medical procedures that involve animal testing.

Vegetarianism is not only an identity with substantial variation but also unstable. According to some research, up to 75 percent of people who try vegetarianism go back to eating meat, and there is some indication that many of them ate some meat even while nominally committed to vegetarianism. Whatever the term *vegetarian* means, it is not a fixed identity.[5]

National and regional identities are similarly unstable. Today our global fusion cuisines change continually and rapidly. But in fact it has always been that way, albeit at a slower pace. Corn, beans, tomatoes, potatoes, eggplant, chocolate, vanilla, and chili peppers were all unknown outside the Americas until the sixteenth century. Once transportation technology was sufficient to encourage trading (and plunder), these foods were rapidly incorporated into traditional cuisines such that today they are inevitably associated with them. Potatoes are now central elements in Indian cooking, and eggplants and chilis help define Thai and Indian cuisine. Tomatoes, eggplant, and potatoes are important to all European cuisines, as is rice, which was imported by the Moorish Arabs when they inhabited southern Spain. It is hard to imagine Italian food without tomatoes, but they did not appear in Neapolitan cookbooks until 1692.

We often think of French cuisine as a kind of cooking that powerfully reflects regional and local identities, and indeed it does up to a point. But the influential French cooking, the dishes that have become well known throughout the world, are for the most part the creations of professional chefs looking for new flavors and textures. Béchamel sauce, created by Louis de Béchamel (1635–1688), was a mainstay of nineteenth- and twentieth-century fine cuisine, although today it is a routine ingredient in comfort food and family dishes, seldom any longer appearing in the recipes of trendsetting chefs. Similarly, sauce béarnaise, crêpes Suzettes, salmon with sorrel sauce, tropical fruit sorbets, and flourless chocolate cakes are all the concoctions of top chefs, as were the creations of nouvelle cuisine that dominated French cooking in the latter half of the twentieth century. Many of the dishes of nouvelle cuisine can now be found in home-style meals. There are some exceptions. Cassoulet, bouillabaisse, foie gras, boeuf bourguignon, and perhaps magret de canard (duck steaks) were regional dishes that achieved international acclaim. But more often than not, change comes about because chefs are experimenting.

Where does this pressure for change come from? Why did Italians embrace the tomato in the sixteenth century, Americans the taco in the twentieth? Why did France abandon heavy spices in the eighteenth century and heavy cream sauces in the twenty-first century in favor of lighter, fresher fare? What encouraged Americans to look to France for culinary inspiration in the 1960s when Julia Child made food TV a habit? Why did virtually the entire globe lose its preference for sweet wine in the mid-twentieth century and begin to embrace the dry styles that now dominate the industry (at least until the current fascination with Moscato)? Why do vegetarians vacillate so much in their sincere commitment?

It is hard to argue that some sort of stable, coherent value system is at work mandating these shifts. Creating taboos, marking national identities, enforcing class distinctions, making moral statements—these are about creating boundaries, not crossing them, about drawing contrasts, not erasing them. Food, by contrast, does a lot of crossing and erasing of boundaries.

Of course there are a lot of explanations for why tastes change. Certainly health considerations, immigration, and socioeconomic factors drive some change—historical change is seldom guided by a single factor. But sometimes change is simply driven by taste. We find new tastes fascinating and want to experience them, and those that are genuinely appealing stick with us until we incorporate them into whatever symbolic identity we happen to be promoting at the time. Of course, then we have to tell some story about why the change is meaningful, not just a matter of taste. Contemporary foodies are doing what we have always done, but with more speed, intensity, and noise, aided by the power of Twitter.

Importantly, all of this change and shape-shifting of identities is incompatible with the judgment that one's way is the right way. If it were the absolutely right way, why would we be so open to change? We are so willing to abandon our foodways that it is hard to take seriously the food flags that people righteously wave. All this change means that there is no such thing as authentic taste if by authenticity we mean a pure origin. Food identities are based on quicksand. The moral eater is showing who she is, but this identity persists only until a new pungency piques her palate. Obviously, we get a kind of emotional fulfillment from all this flag waving and food fighting, but in the end we are chasing flavor. Specific flavors matter, for it is mouth taste driving the moral bus; the flag-waving is a lagniappe, the supporting narrative, an afterthought. Once again, flavors exemplify a sensibility, and it is the sensibility that we love and that is the source of meaning. Flavors are not incidental to the identity-forming narrative but are central to it just as color and line are central to the meaning of a painting.

In the end, we probably can't escape the symbolic dimension of food because symbols are important and food is so readily available to be exploited by our need for meaning. To keep a lid on our passion, it is useful to keep in mind that the power of any particular symbol will persist only until our taste buds object. And then we will have to find a new symbol and manufacture a new passion. Thus, lying at the bottom of this symbolic dimension of food is the power of particular tastes and their ability to shape our moral ideals. If you want people to change their values, change their tastes. Show people that organic broccoli tastes better, and we are on our way to secure their commitment to sustainability. Well, we can hope, can't we?

CONCLUSION

It should be apparent in light of the foregoing, that food's capacity to stand as a symbol of the home, romance, and the sensibility or identity of a culture is not only the product of an external narrative that accompanies the food but also the result of the particular flavors and textures of the food as well. These features are "in the dish" and are central to the meaning that food has. There is in the history of aesthetics a name for this kind of relationship that flavor has to the things it symbolizes—exemplification. The flavors of food show, highlight, or demonstrate what they are trying to say. This relationship of exemplification is precisely what distinguishes meaning in the visual arts. The swirling, tumultuous brush strokes and tense, lurid colors of Munch's *The Scream* exemplify alienation because alienation is often experienced as tumultuous, tense, and unpleasantly harsh and unnatural. This is crucial to the kind of meaning that works of visual art acquire, and what I've tried to show in this chapter is that food can have the same kind of meaning.

The claim that a work of art exemplifies—shows what it is trying to say—was a key component of the aesthetic theory of the mid-twentieth-century philosopher Nelson Goodman, who understood all art as a system of symbols. For Goodman, exemplification is a species of metaphor in which the symbol possesses some of the features of that which it is symbolizing. The flavors of home-cooked meals exemplify "homeyness," the flavor and texture of chocolate or wine exemplify romance, the flavor profile of pesto exemplifies the sensibility of Genoans.[6] Thus, flavors are doing more representational work than the critics of food as art have let on. Flavors and textures are not arbitrary ciphers awaiting a story to acquire meaning—they symbolize, exemplify, and show what they are trying to say. More important, they refer to and serve to highlight the contextual meanings that food has in the celebrations and rituals that give food meaning. Korsmeyer, although explicitly appealing to Goodman's theory of exemplification in explaining the meaning that food acquires, simply misses the crucial role flavors and textures, the aesthetic properties of the food, play in the various narratives that give meaning to food. The cultural prominence of food rests on the secure foundations of robust meaning. The question of what food is about has in part been answered. It is about identity, romance, and the home, and the flavors and textures are performing the referential function.

However, in invoking Goodman's work of symbols, there is one part of his theory that could be fatal to the "food as art" hypothesis if it is not addressed. The problem is that these symbolic meanings that I've mentioned thus far function largely as conventional symbols with relatively fixed meanings. Hence, these examples lack the interpretive open-endedness and robustness of artistic symbols. To use Goodman's terminology, food may lack multiple and complex reference. It is to this issue of the complexity of food meanings that we turn in the next chapter.

6

CAN TUNA CASSEROLE BE A WORK OF ART?

It tastes great, even addicting. The kids love it. The dish is always empty at the end of the pot luck. But it's only tuna casserole. That can't possibly be a work of art, can it? In the previous chapter I argued that food has a variety of meanings that depend not only on a contextual story associated with food but also on the flavors themselves. Yet the residual worry left over from that chapter was that the meanings we associate with food—references to home, personal and cultural identities, and romance—are too conventional and lack the complexity of the meanings we attribute to works of art. If tuna casserole strikes you as an implausible candidate for a work of art, it may well be because it is too ordinary, simple, and old fashioned to carry meanings other than nostalgic yearnings. However, we don't quite have the subject matter of food and beverages in focus yet. Before tuna casserole can be either imbued or relieved of any pretensions to artistic status, we have to know more about the full range of meanings such a commonplace dish can invoke.

The key point in establishing food's credentials as an art is this: Food's capacity for representation is complex, because a dish is a representation of the food tradition from which it emerges, and it bears the marks of that tradition in its flavors, textures, and their arrangement. A preparation of linguine and pesto is a representation of a kind of cooking and eating characteristic of the food traditions of Genoa, Italy. Fried chicken is a representation of certain food traditions from the American South. Burgundian Pinot Noir is a representation of the winemaking traditions of Bourgogne, France. And, yes, tuna casserole is a representation of an approach to food in the United States that became popular in the 1950s when "convenient" was synonymous with "modern." Food represents the taste sensibilities of a people along with the artifacts and culture of food production, eating, and cooking, as they unfold through history, a domain that painting or music would struggle to represent adequately. Thus, the representational capacities of food differ from those of painting or music because they have distinctly different subject matters. After all, no painting, literary work, or musical work can tell us how something tastes. The flavor sensibilities of a people are accessible only via the dishes that exhibit those sensibilities. Those sensibilities, as embedded in traditions, are the subject matter of food and wine, and there is no reason to deny them the rights and privileges of representation in the art world.

The crucial point here is that a dish or meal represents food traditions via its aesthetic properties, the flavors and textures that we taste in the food, not merely through a narrative that we associate with the food. A beef bourguignon represents the tradition of stews made in central France because of the way it tastes. All artistic interpretation depends on context, but just as with a painting such as Munch's *The Scream* described in the previous chapter, edible art reveals context through the aesthetic features of the work, through the flavors and textures that speak so eloquently of the flavor sensibilities of a people. Historical and cultural context is not a mere appendage added to supply meaning, as the skeptic about food as art argues, but is the very subject matter of the work; it is what the flavors, textures, and their arrangement are about. For someone familiar with the sensibility of the tradition, a dish would be meaningful even if she or he were unacquainted with the social narrative of that tradition.

Thus, the flavor arrangement of a dish or meal stands in a particular historical relationship with past arrangements of similar flavors and the cultures that produce and admire them—the flavor arrangement symbolizes and exemplifies that relationship. A particular dish represents, well or badly, the flavor profile of the history of that dish from its region. In fact, the flavors and textures demand interpretation in light of the tradition. The idea that we "read" a plate of food, in the sense that we interpret how the flavors and textures are related to the traditional flavor profiles to which they refer, is neither unintelligible nor nonsensical, for food exhibits through its flavors and textures what it is trying to say.[1] Furthermore, these symbolic references are multiple and complex. Each modification of a dish represents a new way of viewing the tradition from which it emerges. There is substantial complexity in the way recipes quote other recipes, recapitulate and transform flavor themes, and develop dynamically in new directions. Flavors create their own narratives for those who have the discernment to recognize them.

These characteristic meanings that define the edible arts give them intellectual heft, because establishing connections between flavor combinations engages both the imagination and our powers of understanding and insight. When we compare two approaches to gumbo and assess how they succeed or fail to express the distinctive features of southern Louisiana cuisine with its various cultural influences, we engage in the intellectual task of discovering meaning much as a literary or art critic does. To engage in critical practice we must recall and imaginatively compare flavor arrangements, note their complementary and contrasting qualities, assess how the basic elements of the dish are used to form regional structures that add up to a unified whole, and specify the degree to which they are consistent with or subvert the traditional aims of the dish. Thus, the argument that dishes or meals cannot be works of art because they lack multiple and complex, intrinsic meaning does not get off the ground when we properly specify the subject matter of food. Particular culinary masterpieces are representations of food traditions, and culinary artists, through the flavors and textures they create, highlight, interpret, and comment on features of the tradition represented in the food. It is this "aboutness" relationship and the meanings it generates that qualify food as an art form. The same considerations apply to wine as well.

However, despite this rather obvious "aboutness" relationship between particular dishes and food traditions, I suspect there is some residual resistance to the idea that the subject matter of an art is tradition. It is all well and good that food has its own subject matter—food traditions—that supply intrinsic meaning to culinary creations, but surely the mere repetition of the past cannot qualify a dish or meal as a work of art. And what about that tired, hackneyed tuna casserole? Don't we expect an artifact worthy of the honorific title "art" to be innovative, insightful, and, if not beautiful, at least attention grabbing and sensuous? I don't want to prejudge anyone's tuna casserole, but such a dish seems an unlikely candidate.

These are worthy skeptical questions that make an important point. The mere repetition of tradition is not sufficient to create edible art. If desultory cooks have gotten delusions of grandeur from the foregoing, perhaps it's time to deflate expectations. The meals we create during the everyday task of putting food on the table, at home and in most restaurants, may be embedded in food traditions, but they are typically not works of fine art. Most cooks and chefs have no intention of creating works of art, and their patrons will likely be absorbed in conversation rather than mulling over the references to tradition found in the work.

All arts require a practice to sustain them. Without chefs and diners focused on aesthetics, a dish is just a meal. But the same is true of painting or music. Not all paintings or musical works are works of fine art, especially when used outside the practices of the art world as decoration or background. However, the emergence of a serious food culture in the United States and London over the past thirty years to rival some of the more traditional food capitals of Europe and Asia, along with the increasing global attention devoted to food aesthetics on the part of chefs, patrons, and food writers, suggests that such a practice is in place and a genuine art world is under development.

Only when the practice of cooking and eating illuminates, calls attention to, interprets, critiques, or exemplifies, via its aesthetic properties, some dimension of a food tradition are we in the realm of art. Successful works will magnify, glamorize, or ennoble those aesthetic properties, thus calling attention to their meaning as an intervention within a tradition. Even chefs who seek self-expression by fusing ingredients from various traditions are nevertheless making reference to the traditions they are fusing and commenting on their mutability.

Of course, creative chefs need not slavishly follow tradition in order to create edible art. The sincerest form of taking something seriously is to reinterpret, transform, or overcome it. A chef who challenges tradition must be deeply immersed in it, which is why having a classical training is so important in the culinary world. Even the fantastic concoctions of modernist cuisine refer to food traditions. The surprise, playfulness, and deconstructive gestures of their dishes depend on marking a contrast and making reference to the diner's expectations, which are, after all, a product of the traditions that formed their sensibilities. Such food preparations can generate new insights into food traditions; we discover new realms of taste and flavor, new things for a tradition to be, through this kind of innovative cooking. Ferran Adrià, former chef/owner of El Bulli and one of the most innovative chefs on the planet, describes his "deconstructive" approach to cooking:

> It consists of taking a gastronomic reference that is already known, embodied in a dish, and transforming all or some of its ingredients by modifying its texture, shape, and/or temperature. This deconstructed dish will keep its essence and will still be linked to a culinary tradition, but its appearance will be radically different to the original. For this game to be successful, it is essential that the diner has gastronomic memory, since the absence of references turns the concept of deconstruction into mere "construction" based on nothing . . . the result has a direct relationship with the diner's memory, in that although he may not see that he has been served a familiar dish, he later establishes a direct connection between the flavor of what he is eating and the classic recipe; in other words, he recognizes it.[2]

I've focused on the meanings intrinsic to food because arrangements of flavors and textures must have meaning if food is to qualify as art. But the realm of meaning is not restricted to flavors any more than the meaning of a painting is restricted to color or line. All of the dimensions of meaning associated with food—cooking practices, flavor principles, references to home, family, and cultural/moral identity—refer to a set of relationships with people, places, things, and institutions that form a culture with a history that traces that culture's development. When properly prepared and conceptualized, the aesthetic properties of food give us a uniquely powerful mode of access to the world that creates and consumes that food because that world is embodied in the flavors and textures. To the extent that cultural practices are related to food and wine, the flavors in food and wine make reference to these cultural practices and they are part of the world of meaning opened up by the edible arts. One advantage of placing tradition at the center of the edible arts is that it explains the practices of people who take food seriously. Perhaps more so than any other art, people with a deep interest in food are concerned with cultural authenticity and seek out dishes and ingredients that maintain a connection to their origins. Foods made in the traditional way attract a kind of attention not readily found in music or painting. The Slow Food movement, nose-to-tail cooking, seasonal eating, localism, and foraging are some of the food trends that indicate the close connection between food, culture, and tradition. Thus, it is not surprising that tradition would be the subject matter of edible arts, however much it would be less central if we were discussing music or painting. No doubt "tradition" is a difficult word to define precisely, as is "authenticity," a topic to which I turn in the next chapter. However, debates about how to understand traditions are part of the interpretive challenge that food presents, and is no more daunting than the task of defining genres in other artistic media.

BUT IS IT KITSCH?

The idea that we should understand edible art as making reference to food traditions does raise the issue of whether such works might be a form of kitsch. Kitsch art is art that is sentimental or designed to have popular appeal. Its subject matter is easily accessible and thus never challenges the audience. No doubt, the world of food and wine thrives on a heavy dose of nostalgia for an easily accessible past. Culinarians chase down heritage tomatoes, ferment their own vinegar, and learn to butcher hogs in the name of "how things used to be" before the industrial food business created TV dinners and Twinkies. As we scour the Internet for authentic recipes, we imagine simpler times of family farms supporting family feasts consisting of real food, prepared in homey, immaculate kitchens with fruit pies on the windowsill, and the kids shelling beans at the table. Similarly, the wine industry continues to thrive on the romantic myth of the noble winemaker diligently tilling a small vineyard year after year to hand-produce glorious wines that taste of the local soil and climate.

In reality, the winemaking of days past was not so romantic. Bad weather would have ruined some vintages, and difficulties in controlling fermentation temperatures and unsanitary conditions in the winery rendered many wines barely drinkable. As to the way we ate in the not-too-distant past, for most people, food was scarce, expensive, of poor quality, and often unsafe. Kitchens, if they existed, were poorly equipped, and their operation depended on difficult, relentless work by women. Only the wealthy could eat in the manner approaching the quality of contemporary nostalgic yearnings, but that quality usually depended on the work of underpaid kitchen staff after slavery was abolished. Our nostalgic yearnings fail to mention these realities. Nostalgia is a form of selective memory, history without the bad parts, enabling us to enjoy the past without guilt.

Does this dependency on myth render our contemporary fascination with the foods of the past a kind of kitsch—a sentimental, clichéd, easily marketed longing that offers "emotional gratification without intellectual effort" in Walter Benjamin's formulation, an aesthetic and moral failure? Worse, is this longing for the past a conservative resistance to the modern world. The word "nostalgia" has Greek roots—from *nostos* and *algia*, meaning "longing to return home." Are contemporary culinarians and wine enthusiasts longing for a return to the "good" old days?

It should be said that longing for the past is the flipside of our obsession with progress. In this hyper-connected world of instant communication, we most often communicate with people with whom we share few memories, where living together is more or less a recent accident of time and place. We are fascinated with novelty, expecting our browsers to feed us new stimulation every thirty seconds, but the new can become old in a matter of minutes, sucked into the dark matter of history by a new Twitter controversy. In this context, nostalgia arises naturally as an antidote to disconnection and discontinuity, a longing for a less fragmented world where we have more in common with others.

In fact, both our fascination with novelty and our fascination with the past are of recent vintage and deeply entwined. People thoroughly rooted in traditional ways of life would have no need for or access to nostalgia. Whatever losses they would mourn would not be for a different time but for losses suffered within their own time, the only time they know. The idea of tradition is itself a modern invention made possible by our anthropological prowess at unearthing the past, which is now accessible only as institutionalized heritage preserved in museums and monuments. The more distant we are from our past, the more obsessed with tradition we become. Nostalgia is an attempt to patch up the irreversibility of time—to reconstruct a past that is irretrievably gone except as monument and memorial. Of course, this refusal to surrender to the irreversibility of time is itself a modernist impulse. Progress and nostalgia are not antipodes. They need each other. Nostalgia is possible only when progress advances, and progress inevitably creates a heartfelt need for a reconstructed past.

For those uncomfortable with this status-quo-entanglement of nostalgia and progress, two competing visions of a future are salient. For some, the modern world is in a state of arrested disenchantment. Our pursuit of reason and science has succeeded in evacuating intrinsic meaning from the world. The world is a system of causal forces with no aim or purpose;

meaning is something we must invent. But the form of reason available to us to assist in this project of inventing meaning reduces everything and everyone to an instrument, a consumable product, a system in which anything of value can be replaced by something else in the name of efficiency or profit, leaving individuals at the mercy of social forces out of their control. The solution, for those attracted to this hope of progress, is a more complete rationality—one informed by a stronger sense of the common good and human solidarity, a rationally defined utopia that has always been the aim of Enlightenment. That human beings seem incapable of such Enlightenment is a secret passing no one's lips.

To others the modern, disenchanted world is a fabricated world of superficial eye (and ear) candy designed to activate our unconscious sympathies enough to loosen our wallets but doing nothing for our sense of alienation and disconnection. The solution, they argue, is more organic communities rooted in authentic traditions with stable personal relations based on shared values that allow us to wallow in the warmth and comfort of particularistic allegiances.

In this contrast between a more complete science and an organic community, it is not hard to see the stylings of modernist cuisine and the locavore/Slow Food movement as particularly salient examples of this conflict. During the recent past, these two impulses of modernity could be kept separate through the distinction between high and low culture. The fine arts were cosmopolitan and autonomous, mimicking the social role of science in breaking up antiquated traditions and promoting human progress. The folk arts and craftwork, including cooking, were rooted in nostalgia for particularistic communities. With this distinction intact, it was easy to dismiss nostalgia as mere kitsch—easily accessible and comforting but not serious. It was to be hoped that through greater integration of society, as we gradually lose our connection to particularistic traditions, the universal, cosmopolitan impulse would win.

But today, although the Enlightenment project of educating the public via the fine arts still lives in our public rhetoric and on PBS, it looks like a lost cause as symphony orchestras and art programs fall by the wayside. This high culture, in any case, never succeeded in achieving universal appeal, with only a small portion of the educated public attracted to it. The trend in the arts throughout the twentieth century was to break down this distinction between high and low culture by elevating the lowbrow with movements such as Dada and ready-made art objects in the visual arts and rock and jazz in music. But as an agent of change, this too largely fails; the institutions of society have done a good job of commodifying these opposition movements, thus assimilating them to the dead utilitarian world they sought to escape.

Meanwhile, attempts to reimagine authentic particularistic traditions seem dangerous. Nostalgia, by necessity, is the work of imagination, since the real, authentic past is irretrievable. The danger of nostalgia is that it tends to confuse the actual home and the imaginary one. In extreme cases it can create a phantom homeland, for the sake of which one is ready to die or kill. Nostalgia that escapes the realm of imagination can breed monsters.

Of course, the need to invent a past can be an attempt to create feelings of solidarity within a disadvantaged group as they strive for recognition, an understandable and sometimes effective strategy. It can also be placed in the service of powerful elites in society by insulating them from outside influence and making the current power structure seem natural in light of "history." In either case, the aforementioned monsters are lurking. So we have two antagonistic, codependent visions, neither of which is viable. The vision of a perfected future is as implausible as the vision of a perfect past, two false gods at work—Nietzsche was just kidding about *Twilight of the Idols*.

The trick is to get off this dialectic altogether, which is easier said than done. Yet there is a distinction between trying to return to the past in order to rebuild it versus the appropriation of the past as a kind of aesthetic celebration in looking toward the future. After all, it is reasonable when we are heading in the wrong direction to go back to where the mistake was made and clear new pathways. In the end, those seeking a perfected rational society may have no choice but to look to the past for inspiration. In light of the goal of perfection, the present will always seem a failure and thus the future must appear uncertain. Only the past has the stability and certainty to inspire such an ideal. Do modernists dream of electric heirloom tomatoes?

Rather than a simple return to the past, the contemporary fascination with food traditions is a reinterpretation and recontextualization of the past with an eye toward a better-tasting future, much as the rock music traditions of the 1960s reinterpreted the old blues traditions to invent a new form of music. The aim is to imagine an aesthetic ideal that was lost when the food industry conquered all. The threat to meaning doesn't come from a scientific worldview, nor does it come from the lack of a homeland. It comes from the degradation of ordinary life, to which a misguided science or loss of a homeland can contribute. We should view the current food revolution—both the concoctions of modernist cuisine and the nostalgia of the heritage/Slow Food movement—as attempts to re-enchant ordinary life, to make the humble act of preparing food an extraordinary event. Such nostalgia is no longer kitsch but an imaginative attempt to discover a genuine experience, which is what art is supposed to be. The fact we seek such an experience with a tomato perhaps shows how far we've fallen.

RECONSTITUTING ORDINARY LIFE

This discussion of the peculiar role of nostalgia in the food world, brings me to the point that I think lies behind much of the skepticism of food as art. I suppose those who doubt the artistic credentials of food and wine might argue that representations of food and wine traditions are trivial when compared to the areas of life represented by painting or music. After all, themes such as war, social or psychological alienation, love, and the exploration of human emotions are among the themes explored by painting and music. These are monumental themes that penetrate each human life and ramify throughout our existence. In comparison, it is sometimes argued, food seems domesticated, if not small—an everyday function fulfilling merely instinctual needs in a minor arena of life and lacking intellectual import. But an argument that trivializes these small matters appears unmotivated and absurd on its face. The way we relate to the material surfaces of reality is central to human well-being—hardly a trivial matter, and a subject thoroughly explored in the visual and auditory arts. Taking taste seriously does require that we concentrate on the small and transitory, but the small and transitory are, after all, the substance of human life, where most of us live most of the time. We miss much about human existence if we focus only on monumental events, leaving the minutia of everyday life an afterthought.

In fact, of all human activities, the practices surrounding the production and consumption of food may best illuminate the various aspects of culture, for food speaks to the way we produce and consume our material existence. Food preparations exemplify a sensibility, a way of perceiving the material surfaces of reality that marks each culture as distinctive and in part explains our attachment to that culture. When food symbolically represents these dimensions of culture, it makes reference to something essential to our lives.

But this exposes the central tension in the food revolution's elevation of food to an art form. This tension can be stated in the form of a paradox—treat food as an art and it becomes disconnected from the ordinary, everyday contexts in which it has comfortably resided for centuries, and gets much of its meaning. Treat it as a craft, as a form of everyday aesthetics, and its development is likely to stagnate and lose the critical edge it has gained within culture.

Yet there is reason to think there is more continuity between fine cuisine and home cooking that lessens the tension between food as art and food as a source of everyday pleasure. In *Culture and Cuisine: A Journey through the History of Food*, Jean-Jacques Revel writes:

> Cuisine stems from two sources: a popular one and an erudite one. . . . In the course of history there has been a peasant (or seafarer's) cuisine and a court cuisine; a plebeian cuisine and a family cuisine prepared by the mother (or the humble family cook); and a cuisine of professionals that only chefs fanatically devoted to their art have the time and the knowledge to practice. . . . The history of gastronomy is nothing more nor less than a succession of exchanges, conflicts, quarrels, and reconciliations between everyday cuisine and the high art of cuisine. Art is a personal creation, but this creation is impossible without a base in traditional craftsmanship.[3]

The cuisine of the less-well-off is linked to the soil and climate of a particular region and is based on skills and flavor combinations that have stood the test of time. Chefs of fine cuisine must innovate and go beyond traditions, but those who ignore traditions entirely engage in "pointless complication" and seldom create anything "really exquisite," according to Revel.

Since the eighteenth century, and the emergence of a well-off middle class with access to media, these two cuisines have been mediated by a "bourgeois cuisine," which "retains the heartiness and savor of peasant cuisine" while introducing some of the subtleties and innovation of haute cuisine. (This mediation accelerated in the twentieth century with media figures such as Julia Child.)

Both were necessary. Without professional innovation, food traditions would stagnate and endlessly repeat mistakes. But without everyday cuisine, professional cooking runs the risk of creations that are "pointlessly complicated" and "at once extravagant and dull," enlivened only by the importing of incongruous ingredients that eventually create a uniform international style.

Revel's attempt to make sense of culinary history was written in 1982—before the Internet, the Food Network, the growing role of science in the kitchen, and thirty years of increased population movements around the globe accelerated the fragmentation of traditions. Does Revel's account of how great cuisine is created still hold? Today there is a continuous circulation of culinary ideas that pays little attention to geographical borders. Every meal is a mash-up. Chefs are in the driver's seat, deciding what should be prepared and using new forms of media and their celebrity to instantaneously transmit it across the globe, where it can be copied and circulated again and again, with simplified versions filtering into "bourgeois" cuisine until it all becomes quickly obsolete and replaced with the new sensation.

Although a sense of history is often used to promote these new creations, history is itself constantly reinvented and recontextualized so that it functions only as a nostalgic symbol, not as a standard. Thus "novelty" is never quite novelty. Since everything is always new, the new doesn't mark a new direction but only a difference to be noted and then discarded to make room for the new difference to take its place. There is lots of movement but no direction.

My worry is that without tradition we cannot understand what is an advance and what is a regression. Traditions provide a context that enables interpretation. They provide meaning and direction to innovations that give rise to the judgment "X tastes better than Y." There is something that a particular dish is supposed to taste like that can be shown to be inferior when supplanted by something truly innovative rather than simply different. Thus, tradition is the handmaiden, not the enemy, of novelty. So Revel's insight remains true. We need home cooking to supply the discipline that anchors innovation.

As the food revolution has unfolded, chefs have become not only celebrities but also role models for home cooks to emulate. Their advice for home cooks blankets the Internet and Food Network, and it is disseminated in large, very expensive cookbooks replete with all the staging of an art show catalog, with recipes using ingredients that require a good detective to find. After all, they are the experts. Who better to learn from than people who have devoted their lives to the pursuit of flavor? So we watch them construct glorious meals in thirty minutes and buy their cookbooks hoping that all that expertise will rub off on our rushed and ill-planned everyday meals. "Knowing how to cook" has come to mean "knowing how to cook like Grant Achatz or Thomas Keller." It is ironic that as people have less time to cook and few are inclined to bother, the standards for what counts as good cooking have ratcheted up.

I must plead guilty to this "mission creep." I've worked my way through the *French Laundry Cookbook*, dabbled in molecular gastronomy, and been known to spend the better part of a week preparing a meal. But this is terribly unrealistic, and I feel less and less inclined to go to so much trouble. Fine cuisine really has become an art form, but that has put fine cuisine out of the reach of time- and budget-limited home cooks. More important, in adopting the standards of a restaurant chef, we risk diminishing the importance of everyday cooking. Home cooking and restaurant food have very different goals and embody very different values. Home cooking is about sustenance, family bonds, and everyday pleasures—the kind of pleasure that can spice up our lives every hour. The accessibility of everyday pleasures, their constant availability, is what is essential about them. Restaurant food is about complexity, originality, and artful presentation using ingredients and techniques that are special precisely because they are unavailable to us at home. It is their rarity and inaccessibility that contributes to their value. We go to restaurants to eat what we can't eat at home and be dazzled by the unfamiliar.

Both restaurant and home cooks aim to maximize flavor, both aim to please others and create an atmosphere of conviviality (although the restaurant chef will have less personal connection to diners), both take the potential of food seriously and seek to make it the center of experience, but they do so in very different contexts with very different constraints. The advice of professionals is often useful when it makes us more efficient, but we need to keep in mind the differences.

This is not to say that home cooks should not be creative. But it is the practical, find-something-interesting-to-do-with-what-you-have-and-can-afford kind of creativity that home cooks need. This is the real value of amateur and semi-pro food blogs. They are a cauldron of ideas from people who must take the limits of time, equipment, knowledge, and money into account. It is they who should set the standards for home cooking, as the old family traditions of home cooking continue to erode. But the celebrity chefs have an important role to play. Without virtuoso performances cooking will lack direction, for it has always been restaurant chefs who have the resources to be creative without the constraints that limit the home cook. This is what makes a chef such as Rene Redzepi of Nomi so fascinating. He focuses intensely on Danish cooking, relentlessly searching for local ingredients, wild and domesticated, to enhance his dishes; that focus enables him to find new things for Danish cooking to be. We look to these virtuoso performances for inspiration and ideas but it is the home cook who must translate them into a form appropriate for everyday use, thereby securing a dish's place in its tradition.

Despite the attention celebrity chefs receive, and their important role in driving cooking forward, the heart of the food revolution is still in the home. Among nonprofessionals, labor intensive projects are valued as a means of expressing or redefining the self, of bringing intensity and joy to living, and as a form of resistance to the relentless pace of life in our work-obsessed culture. As I have been arguing, this resistance explains why we have undergone a food revolution in this country. Whatever other virtues it may have, the increasingly corporate, bureaucratic, pressurized world of work is not a place for self-expression, authenticity, creativity, or care. The world of food and wine is our contemporary retreat from all of that—a place where the intrinsic value of the joys of life can be celebrated daily. It's the kind of modest revolution that may not make the history books but immeasurably improves peoples' lives.

However, when we strive to take ordinary objects like a tuna casserole and give them significance as a mode of self-expression and creativity, we are lifting them out of the realm of the commonplace to something that is unusual or striking. In other words, when we successfully make something worthy of aesthetic attention, we make it extraordinary and a candidate for consideration as a work of art. Philosopher Tom Leddy, in his book *The Extraordinary in the Ordinary*, wonders "whether it is possible to approach the ordinariness of the ordinary without making it extraordinary, without approaching it, therefore, in an art-like way."[4]

Indeed, when we try to make a dish that is immensely satisfying to our guests and also a form of creative self-expression, the distinction between home cook and chef is less than clear, for we are making the ordinary extraordinary just as professional chefs are. As Leddy writes, "The ordinary qua ordinary is uninteresting or boring and only becomes aesthetic when transformed" to become something like a work of art. In fact, as Leddy points out, most art begins with the everyday. Artists regularly take objects from ordinary life and transfigure them "first in the perception and then through their art-making."[5] In Leddy's view, ordinary objects merit our attention because of their "aura," by which he means an object has "the quality of heightened significance in which it seems to extend beyond itself"—experiencing an object in a particularly vivid way so it seems more real and alive. "Aura is what aesthetic properties have in common" and is shared by works of art as well as those ordinary objects that are worthy of special attention and that give us pleasure.[6] Making an aesthetic judgment involves singling something out as being different from and having more significance than other run-of-the-mill objects and ascribing aesthetic properties to it. Can a tuna casserole be a work of art? Indeed it can if it has features that make it stand out from the crowd, not merely as being the best of what is on offer but also as standing out from the ordinary.

Thus, there can be no sharp distinction between works of art and everyday objects like home-cooked culinary creations that strike us as extraordinary. We come to grasp the "aura" of things more readily through the medium of art and thus great chefs have a role to play in enhancing our ability to recognize and understand extraordinary culinary creations. However, there is nothing in the nature of home cooking that precludes a home cook from creating works of art if she or he is imaginative enough to imbue those creations with aura.

In summary, just as the *Mona Lisa* is about a particular model, her enigmatic smile, and a sense of mystery encouraged by the ethereal ambiance of the painting, food and wine are about food traditions and the social traditions that encompass them. Particular dishes provide an interpretation of a food tradition, and their flavors and textures give us insight into that tradition and its sensibility, fissures, debates, and limitations, all of which supply a depth of intellectual content that rivals the other fine arts. Perhaps we can look forward to the day when we visit the art museum to sample Myhrvold with our Monet, although it is to be hoped the price of admission to our temples of gastronomy will not survive that transplantation.

Is your tuna casserole a work of art? Are you commenting on or interpreting a food tradition in a way that provides depth and insight? Are you magnifying, glamorizing, or ennobling the aesthetic features of canned tuna? Is noble canned tuna an oxymoron?

7

HABITS AND HERESIES

Authenticity, Food Rules, and Tradition

If any word has become the talisman of the food revolution, where its incantation can confer instantaneous legitimacy, it is the word *authentic*. The word is ubiquitously splattered across menus and throughout cookbooks. It screams from neon signs and crosses the lips of every foodie who wishes to criticize a restaurant not up to standards. The ability to cook with authenticity is a source of regional or national pride for aspiring chefs. There are food rules that indicate authenticity, and woe to the unsuspecting philistine who violates them.

I argued in the previous chapter that dishes are a representation of the food tradition from which they emerge. But what counts as an authentic representation of a tradition, and who decides? All of us come to the table with a history of eating experiences that have left behind a sediment of preferences, a map of what goes with what, an impressionistic bible of what particular ingredients should taste like and how particular dishes satisfy. Food is the constant companion present when love emerges, deals are made, and sorrow weighs. Thus, food memories meld with emotional cues and are appended to the minor and major ceremonies that constitute the routines of life. Flavors acquire an emotional resonance and symbolic power that enables them to express the style of a culture and provide some of the prohibitions and taboos that signify social boundaries and status. There is a right and wrong way to eat, and if you get it wrong, you cannot be one of us.

Just as linguistic meaning is encoded in physical inscription (writing) and phonemes (speaking), food meanings are encoded in the flavors and textures with which people identify, a semi-consciously held template that says Italian, French, or low country. This template cannot be fully articulated in a set of rules; one knows the taste of home even if one can't say what home tastes like. Although the original association of flavors with identities is arbitrary, conventional, and driven by accidents of geography, once established they are no longer arbitrary but consciously perpetuated via resemblance. Cooks working within food traditions create dishes that replicate that template because their patron's map and bible generate those expectations. The relationship between flavor and meaning is not merely an association but also a synthesis. Moral taste and mouth taste become one. When a server puts a plate of food in front of you, the dish confronts your map and bible. The dish may or may not represent your tradition, may or may not represent your map and bible, but it represents some tradition or other and expresses someone's style, thus posing a question about where and how it fits. The dish refers to other dishes as an imitation, interpretation, challenge, or affront. Is it an authentic extension of the tradition or a violation worthy of scorn?

What gives food traditions their staying power and capacity for repetition? Is it like a bad habit, something we've fallen into and repeat unthinkingly, or do they have some real authority? The fact that deviations from the norm are often met with derision, disgust, and hostility suggests that food traditions have genuine normative authority. They acquire such authority because they express one's cultural identity. Our self-concept is in part derived from perceived membership in a culture—eating a particular style of food, as a matter of habit, is for some people a condition of membership and a badge of authenticity. But, more important, food traditions embody familiar flavors served in familiar ways, and familiarity has its own deeply felt emotional resonance, especially when it involves taking something into our bodies. Food is a constant necessity and its procurement and consumption requires a robust social context, so it is deeply woven with our history and emotions, and it is naturally associated with a sense of "at homeness," of location, and intimacy. Food rules have normative authority because their violation is an affront to our self-concept and threatens our implicit sense of security that we expect from food. If you're Italian, don't eat cheese with fish or have coffee during dinner. If you're French, never eat salad before the main dish. Pennsylvanians know you can't get a decent cheesesteak in any other state; transplanted New Yorkers would give up pizza rather than eat that stuff from Chicago; and to a Texan any other barbecue does not even count as meat. Transgressors be warned. Thus, culinary travelers take authenticity, strict conformity to the map and bible, to be a central aesthetic consideration. Only when eating the "real thing" does one gain access to that realm of intimacy and location. But all this vehemence rings false.

As I explained in chapter 5, food fights raise a paradox. The prevalence of food rules and the rhetoric of authenticity suggest that any transgression is met with disapproval. But history tells a different story, one of unstable identities and porous cultural boundaries rendering debates about authenticity interminable and pointless. It was not until the end of the nineteenth century that olive oil became essential to the cooking of southern France. Pizza and pasta were originally eaten only in southern Italy. Tomatoes, corn, beans, peppers, and potatoes, all staples of European cooking, had their origins in the New World. If identities are based on food preferences, those identities are ceaselessly changing. Today, anyone with resources can eat almost anything they want if they have a computer and a shipping address. The maps and bibles are so tattered they seem incapable of supporting the vitriol spilled in their name. Given their shabby condition, why do food fights arise in the first place? Why worry about authenticity at all?

Identities, whether based on food or some other characteristic, are unstable because they confront a variety of oppositions that have already mounted an invasion and taken hostages. An explicitly articulated, self-conscious identity is not something one needs unless that identity is under threat, when trespassers have already taken their liberties. When identity requires continual assertion because it is persistently being challenged, it must be consciously held and forcefully asserted. At that point, the concept of authenticity becomes decisive. One needs some way of separating what is really theirs from the impostors who have crossed the border. Thus, food becomes a symbol of pride and contest. The British love of beef, in part, gets its authority from its ability to mark a difference from the French, who don't consider beef essential. But this would not be necessary unless French cuisine had not already gained a foothold among the British. Italians differentiate themselves from and even look down on others because of their belief that no one eats as well as they do, but only because they have been fighting encroachments from the Mediterranean and northern Europe for centuries. Nouveau Mexican high cuisine is a reaction to the hijacking of Mexican food by global industrial food corporations. Food fights presuppose a contest that makes the assertion of identity necessary, defining oneself via a contrast with what one is not, as different from the other. But the other is setting the agenda, forcing the issue. Flavors cross borders easily and the attractions of food-induced pleasure, even when foreign and unfamiliar, are hard to resist, authenticity notwithstanding. The battle is joined after the war is lost.

Traditions represent a common stock of knowledge and use rituals, symbols, and ceremonies to link people to a place, a common sense of the past and a sense of belonging. But at the same time, the idea of local culture is a relational concept and the act of drawing a boundary a relational act that depends on situating oneself within a network of other localities that already have exerted influence. Modern food identities, in fact, must reverberate in two directions. They must unify a region or country and give it prominence on the world stage while relentlessly focusing on the local. This is why pasta is such a powerful national symbol for the Italians. It is ubiquitous in every part of Italy and has become the dominant symbol of Italian food. Yet the particular shape and texture of pasta is governed by an array of local norms that determine which shapes are to be used and with what condiment, thus providing a cultural boundary to identify outsiders.

In contemporary life, this assertion of identity has taken an interesting turn. The greatest threat to all food traditions, and the identities they support, is the increasing homogenization of food, as global food corporations expand across the globe. The ubiquitous hamburger, especially as interpreted by McDonald's and a plethora of other fast-food chains, Coca-Cola and other soft drinks, snack foods, and processed foods made identically by global corporations are common in every industrialized nation on the globe. In chain restaurants, novelty and surprise are minimized. The decor and menus must be familiar, with only minor adjustments made to accommodate local tastes, and interactions with the consumer are scripted regardless of locale. Today in major cities across the globe virtually any food can be found anywhere with no connection to a particular location, often in combinations that juxtapose many cuisines on the same plate. Even haute cuisine is threatened by homogenization, with pricey restaurants from New York to London to Tokyo serving very similar dishes to a business class seeking familiarity. The culinary traveler can remain at home and find most of what she or he can imagine. Thus, today, the authority of tradition comes from its ability to assert distinctiveness in the face of this homogenization. Food identities root us in the local and particular as opposed to the global, homogenized, bureaucratic world, and authenticity is perceived as a cure for excessive homogenization. Modern food identities presuppose a discourse of taste that implies that "natural," rooted, artisanal products taste better than mass-produced ones. Furthermore, knowing the producer adds an imaginary value to the food that helps it to taste better. The fact that a particular person made it contributes to its quality because it is seen as a genuine expression of that person's identity.

But we return to the problem. What counts as genuinely authentic, embodying a real awareness of actual history and geography? Too often appeals to authenticity select only portions of the past to remember and what is remembered is highly idealized, as manufactured as the corporate food it seeks to displace. Unfortunately, any return to the past will be a narrative reinvention—an account of the past as it looks to us after the fact, satisfying a need for romance and imagination, but having little connection to "how it really was."

Before the emergence of mass transportation, food cultures had essential properties determined by the necessities of agriculture and geography. Today food cultures are more imaginary—ways of constructing opposition and projecting strength. So they must react and be negotiated. There is no pure past available for the taking—all memory is influenced by the living present. This means that traditions must change because they are continually confronted by new threats, encroachments, copiers, and pretenders, and so they must find new ways of asserting identity.

This is where the chef as artist comes into play performing the delicate balance between innovation and tradition. Restlessness toward the status quo is essential to being an artist. They may be inspired by the past but their aim is seldom simply to emulate it. Any work of art is an experiment that strives to reach beyond what has been done. However, the artist's audience will be the ultimate arbiter of success and the culinary artist is no exception. Chefs must negotiate their way through maps and bibles— the expectations of diners. In the edible arts, awareness of tradition is essential and must be preserved.

Innovative dishes thus pose a question: Is it authentic? Are the violations of tradition that give a dish its originality and excitement indicative of the proper direction for that tradition? There is tension between chef and patron. The creative chef revels in the detour, whereas customers want a straighter line, a place of respite, an end that is still recognizable according to their map and bible. How do chefs and cooks work through this conflict?

We need to question the very notion of authenticity that is presupposed by the conflict. Why should "authentic" mean that a dish is prepared exactly the way an insider from the past would have cooked it, especially when it is likely that insiders in the past did a lot of experimenting in responding to their local conditions. Every Italian grandmother will tell you she has a secret recipe for some staple dish that makes it utterly unique. But that conceit can possess a modicum of truth only if Italian grandmothers were experimenting, trying new approaches with the ingredients they had available. Who has the authentic recipe? There isn't one. There are as many authentic recipes as Italian grandmothers.

Furthermore, even if we could agree that a dish was prepared in an authentic manner using authentic ingredients, why think a diner has the ability to experience it as authentic? As noted, diners come to a dish with a history of experience that shapes their perception of it. People from outside a culture—or insiders who have had extensive experience as culinary travelers themselves—are unlikely to experience a dish in the same way as an indigenous, historical diner did since they have vastly different experiences—a different map and bible. A work of cuisine is a different work for the cultural insider in contrast to the culinary traveler. Whatever authenticity means, it cannot mean a pure origin that can repeat itself over and over without variation.

Who gets to assert the authority of authenticity, insider or outsider, the indigenous cook or the diasporic cook? The diaspora represents a danger. It may be utterly cut off from the history, traditions, and ingredients of the homeland and thus inventions may lack any continuity with an original tradition. Transgression is easier in the diaspora because it may be divorced from the experiences that gave rise to historical pressures to assert an identity. However, the diaspora can also represent multiple directions and modes of representation. Diasporic communities must try to make a difference within their cultures of residence often amid a good deal of hostility. Thus, the diasporic cook is located between two histories and must invent a narrative in active relationship with the native culture. Furthermore, a historical reality wedded to a place of origin is not more "natural" or "authentic" than the experience of people who have been displaced and must create a plural identity. Diasporas are too real to be dismissed as aberrations—the connection between home and diaspora must be relational, with neither having the authority to speak for the other.

The border crossings that inevitably disrupt narratives of authenticity are perhaps best illustrated by the story of Mexican food, ably told by Jeffrey Pilcher in his book *Planet Taco*.[1] Is your neighborhood Mexican restaurant in LA, Minneapolis, or New York authentic? As Pilcher describes, they likely serve tacos that were probably invented by Mexican silver miners and gradually became identified with Mexico City street food. But in the mid-twentieth century, Mexican Americans in the Southwest began to fill them with hamburger, cheddar cheese, iceberg lettuce, and tomato because these were available in their local supermarket. Were they being inauthentic? Glen Bell of Taco Bell fame claims to have invented the hard shell taco, but Mexican cookbooks show tortillas being folded over and fried at least a decade before Bell's patent. Thus, even that symbol of industrial food may have a more authentic origin than is generally acknowledged. And if you prefer Tacos Al Pastor, now popular throughout the United States and Mexico, you're probably eating a version of the taco invented in the 1950s by Middle Eastern immigrants to Mexico who cooked pork on a vertical spit shwarma-style and put it on a corn tortilla with a slice of pineapple.

Your neighborhood Mexican restaurant also is likely to serve burritos; yet they are seldom eaten in Mexico. At best they may date back to the late nineteenth century in northern Mexico, where wheat was grown and transformed into flour tortillas, but they were never a prominent part of the diet. They became part of California Mexican food because they were popular along the contemporary U.S.-Mexican border. They are, in a sense, distinctly American because it was Mexican Americans who decided they must be made with flour tortillas. In northern Mexico they were likely eaten with both corn and wheat tortillas.

Purists often dismiss this so-called border food as inauthentic. But why? People who lived along the Mexican/American border have their own food traditions that are worthy of celebration and elaboration. Whether a food is authentic or not crucially depends on the question—authentic for whom? Since the Mexican/American border regions are made up of land and populations stolen by the United States in an attempt to expand slavery, it hardly makes sense to exclude the indigenous cuisines of the border states as lacking authenticity. What is authentic are people reformulating their recipes to take advantage of whatever ingredients they have available. This is how food traditions have always developed.

TWO MEANINGS OF AUTHENTICITY

Part of the difficulty with the whole debate about authenticity is that there are at least two primary definitions of authenticity. In contemporary debates about food the two definitions are often conflated. We use the term "authentic" to describe something whose origins have been correctly determined—the authenticity of historical accuracy. A painting is an authentic Rembrandt if it was indeed painted by Rembrandt, not a forgery or a copy. A dish or recipe would be authentic, in this sense, if it were identical to some original version of it. In the culinary world, there are many reasons why we might value authenticity of this sort—we might want to understand the sensibility of historical people or seek to understand how a dish was related to the culture in which it first appeared. We might want to know why people found it attractive or to recapture something of the history of taste that is in danger of disappearing.

From an aesthetic point of view, we view originals as having more value than copies or forgeries because it is the original that constitutes the achievement. We value an original painting by Rembrandt more than an identical copy because it is the original that represents the struggles and insights that led to its creation—the copy has none of those associations regardless of how attractive it may be. Similarly, we value a traditional dish or recipe because it was actually a part of people's lives, a companion to their hopes, dreams, or tragedies.

However, it is crucial to note the ways in which culinary preparations differ from paintings. When viewing one of Rembrandt's self-portraits in the Metropolitan Museum of Art, you are in the presence of the actual object that Rembrandt painted. No doubt the paint is now cracked and faded and the painting is in a museum rather than Rembrandt's studio, but nevertheless we witness the very object itself. The art of cooking can claim no such direct acquaintance with artifacts of the past. We may have a recipe, a set of instructions about how to prepare a dish, but recipes are rendered differently by individual cooks, and, as noted above, the mixing of populations and the liberties taken by individual cooks make it difficult to determine a single "authentic" version of a dish. Furthermore, ingredients may no longer be available or may taste differently today when grown under vastly different geographical or climatic conditions. In addition, cooking utensils and appliances are made from different materials than in the past. But most important, our map and bible is utterly different from that of historical people. We are accustomed to different foods and so any judgment about what it was like to eat something from the past will be in comparison to a vastly different diet.

This problem with historical reconstruction is not unique to the culinary arts. Musicologists face similar problems because original works of music, prior to the advent of recordings, could be preserved only in a musical score that gives instructions to performers, much like a recipe. Individual performers will have different interpretations of the score. Changes in the technology of musical instruments make it similarly difficult to reconstruct the experience of musical works as historical people would have heard them. Just as in the world of music there are attempts to reconstruct past listening experiences as best we can, there are similar attempts in the food world. But these are largely matters for food historians and anthropologists to pursue. Only on rare occasions could a restaurant undertake to reconstruct a dish with unerring historical accuracy. Outside academic contexts the pursuit of authenticity understood as the correct origin of a dish is a fantasy—or just marketing.

Are gastrophiles who seek authenticity on a quest that can never be realized? It is tempting to disown the whole idea of authenticity because in the contemporary world authenticity isn't authentic. The quest for authenticity is endlessly appropriated by large corporations who claim to advance artisanal values and deck themselves out in the trappings of old-world romance and compassionate service, their franchisees often hiding their affiliation with the larger company. Authenticity has become just another selling point, a marketing ploy to fool unwitting customers, or it is preserved in mothballs by governments who fear the old ways of cooking and eating are disappearing. In 1993, the European Union introduced a framework for granting protected status to certain dishes and products that prevents them from being copied and appropriated by other localities. Thus, only the sparkling wine produced in Champagne can be called "Champagne," and only Parmesan cheese made in Reggiano can be called "Parmesan Reggiano." And the United Nations, via UNESCO, has placed certain cuisines on their Representative List of the Intangible Cultural Heritage of Humanity, which has general specifications for defining these cuisines. But these attempts to preserve heritage cannot accommodate new developments in cuisines, and decisions are often politically motivated, designed more to promote tourism and trade than to preserve an authentic history.

But giving up on the idea of authenticity would be a hasty concession to the forces of the production paradigm, which would be happy to see truth swallowed up in the pursuit of profit. The search to find something situated in its place and time, a source of direct contact and unmediated communication, may be an old idea, but it is one with increasing resonance as our hold on place and time slips away. People seek authenticity because they want to take care of their needs without the loss of freedom entailed by socially dysfunctional corporations. The pursuit of what is real is not likely to lose its attraction regardless of how much the propagandists laugh.

Happily, there is another meaning of the word "authentic" that is more readily achieved—we might call this "expressive authenticity."[2] It means, essentially, being true to oneself, not being derivative or copying someone else's way of doing something. Such authenticity requires a commitment to one's personal expression rather than to an historical tradition, although one could view continuity with tradition as essential to one's personal expression. Philosophers will recognize this kind of authenticity in the writings on the subject by existentialists such as Jean-Paul Sartre and Martin Heidegger. This, I would argue, is the kind of authenticity we care about when we criticize a restaurant's food for lacking authenticity—there is something manufactured, factitious, or fake about it. It claims to be something it is not. How do we recognize food that is inauthentic, factitious, or fake?

To get to the bottom of expressive authenticity, it would be helpful to suspend discussion of food for a moment and think about how we deal with this issue in other arenas. Blues is a musical form that is widely considered an authentic expression of African American culture in the United States. It has its origins in the spiritual music of nineteenth-century slaves, and the traditions of American blues have a continuous development that can be traced from this spiritual music through the music of southern blacks such as Mississippi John Hurt or Robert Johnson. Yet in the 1950s and 1960s American blues changed dramatically. Electrical instruments were introduced, recordings became a common medium for listening, and the music thus received wider distribution. Although rock 'n' roll had evolved from and was deeply influenced by the blues traditions, newly created rock idioms and techniques began to feed back into the development of the blues, and white performers, most notably from England, such as Eric Clapton and John Mayall, become central figures claiming continuity with this tradition. Importantly, the audience for this music had shifted substantially. Earlier incarnations of the blues were directed to other members of the African American community. But gradually, the blues acquired a white audience as well. Were these white performers authentic blues players or pretenders engaged in cultural misappropriation?

No doubt there were examples of cultural misappropriation. But many of these white performers were able to master the subtle expressive details of the guitar work or vocal mannerisms of African American performers. There were clear differences in sound, especially in vocal timbre, and the ethos of romantic individualism, which characterized the world of rock music, gave license to performers to add their own personal dimension. Yet an analysis of the music—melodic and harmonic structure, rhythmic patterns and musical textures—shows broad continuity between this new approach to the blues and the blues traditions. The fact that many black performers were embracing the electric guitar and some of the rock rhythmic patterns made this continuity easier to discern. [3]

However, the question of cultural expression is the sticking point. The blues traditions were an expression of the nature of life in the African American community, the hardships and trials, the confrontation with racism, the life rhythms of the rural South or, later, the inner-city ghettos. White players from the suburbs of Chicago or the working-class neighborhoods of Birmingham, England, were at some distance from the cultural milieu of the black community, although many of them saw themselves as dealing with their own forms of oppression and alienation. In any case, they lived vastly different lives. How, then, could these new developments in blues be seen as having cultural continuity with the past incarnations of the blues firmly rooted in African American communities?

To be sure, these questions of authenticity caused a good deal of conflict within the blues community. Many African Americans saw the white performers as interlopers and their audiences as engaged in a cheap form of cultural tourism, helping themselves to the satisfactions of the music without experiencing the hardships and joys of life in the black community. Yet not all viewed these new performers and audiences in a negative light. Many, especially the black musicians themselves, admired some of the white players for their skill and dedication to the music, and some viewed the expansion of the audience for blues as opening up opportunities for the growth of blues as an art form.

Without minimizing the very real conflicts that inevitably accompany such cultural appropriation, it nevertheless seems fair to say that to the extent that white players were able to master the subtleties of the musical idioms that constitute playing the blues, and thereby communicate the emotional content of the music, they were an authentic extension of the blues tradition. When they brought a new sensibility to the music through individual creativity they were expanding the expressive possibilities of that music by showing that the feelings evoked by the blues were human feelings that could be heartfelt despite lacking rootedness in the original community. For those players who took continuity with the blues tradition seriously, there was nothing in their approach that was in conflict with the values of the originating community. (This, of course, was not true of all white blues players if they lacked respect for the traditions they were appropriating.)

Thus, the question about the authenticity of electric-based white blues is not about its conformity to an origin. Neither electric instruments nor white performers were there at the birth of the blues. What seems to matter here is the personal commitment of the players to continuity with the blues tradition and the degree to which their personal expression via the music showed evidence of that personal commitment. Thus, it should be emphasized that a connection to history is not irrelevant to expressive authenticity. But what matters is not fidelity to an origin but rather a commitment to continuity. To be taken seriously as part of the blues tradition, electric blues players had to preserve key elements of the harmonic and melodic structure as well as the expressive idioms of that tradition. As Dutton notes, judgments about expressive authenticity involve attention to "the larger artistic potential" of a work. An authentic performance is one "in which the aesthetic potential . . . is most fully realized." Thus, expressively authentic works can express unforeseen meanings and new directions that go beyond the intention of the original, raising questions about whether what we find in a new direction is appropriate, given the original meanings, and whether audiences are likely to understand these new directions. Expressive authenticity is under constant development, not established by an origin at the work's creation but constituted by a work's ability to accommodate change and continue to make itself intelligible without losing its center.

The element of personal commitment is decisive. Works of art express both the cultural beliefs of a people as well as the sensibility of individual artists. We are interested in art because of its capacity for such multifaceted expression, and part of the meaning of a work is the degree to which it is continuous with some tradition. In addition, the sincerity and passion with which artists undertake their work is part of what we find attractive about it, and in evaluating the work we seek evidence of that passion and commitment. The artist's intentions and the quality of her or his practice in its commitment to expressing the values of a tradition are what matters. This is why the issue of commercialism will arise in this debate. To the extent that an artist is focused on making money instead of extending the expressive possibilities of a tradition, she or he lacks the proper intentions to claim authenticity. This is not to say that commercially successful artists cannot be authentic—only that some commercially successful artists can lose their intention to advance a tradition or engage in self-expression if they make too many compromises, and thus their authenticity can be challenged.

Expressive authenticity does not require that a work be identical to some original version or that it strictly conform to the past. But it does require that a work express the values of the artist including the values shared by the historical community with which the artist identifies. Authenticity in this sense is as future focused as it is focused on the past, for the aim is to project a tradition into the future in a way that preserves its vitality. Expressive authenticity lacks the simplicity of authenticity based on historical origins. Whether something is an original or not can be established as a fact. Establishing the expressive authenticity of a work requires a complex interpretation that takes into consideration intentions, audience, and aesthetic potential, none of which can be established without controversy.

AUTHENTIC FOOD

Let's return to food and the appeals to authenticity that are so extant today in the world of food. A dish, recipe, or approach to cooking is authentic if the cooks or chefs have gone to the trouble to learn the techniques and flavor profiles that constitute the tradition they are working in so that changes are viewed as an organic development of that tradition. In their practice, they care about the vitality of the tradition. They have made a commitment to show continuity with the tradition, preserving key elements when they can and making only those changes that can be viewed as continuous. In doing so, the meanings that attach to the tradition, the resonance with memory, the mark of the centrality of key ingredients, and the "flavors of home" are still available as a matter of interpretation. The intention to be genuine is there and can be sensed in their approach. The food has work to do; it must evoke the rhythms of life associated with the people whose tradition it is. When you eat, for example, a machaca burrito made in the traditional way by people who trace their heritage to Sonora, Mexico, you are experiencing a representation of the sensibility of a particular group of historical agents. The representation is all the more vivid when consumed in a place and with people who have a historical connection to the original. Is it a representation, a facsimile? Of course. As I noted above, we cannot return to a pure origin. But there is a vast difference between eating a burrito at El Charro in Tucson and eating one at Disneyland because the meanings and associations in Tucson will show more continuity with the traditions of Sonoran-style Mexican food than what you are likely to find in the shadow of the "Matterhorn."

This is why artisanal foods, locally produced and in limited quantities, are more likely to be authentic in the expressive sense of that term. Care to preserve continuity with a tradition, to stay close to the sensibility of a particular local culture, and to produce food that creates the associations that make food meaningful is more likely when the pressures of efficiency, profit, and shareholder dividends are not the primary motivation. Standardization and commercialization are not compatible with these goals of a genuine artisan, and thus we are unlikely to find authenticity in chain stores and franchise operations. A friend recently reminded me that Starbucks, the ubiquitous chain of coffee shops, was once a small artisan coffee roaster located in Seattle and asked me, "Should we fall out of love with them because they've grown?" The short answer is yes. As much as they have contributed to putting quality coffee on the map in the United States, they can no longer claim to be sensitive to local sensibilities or to avoid the dreaded monotony of standardization.

Crucially, just as in the case of music, audience matters. Instead of insisting that dishes be prepared the way they historically have been prepared in their native context, we should endorse cooks who recognize the limitations of their diners, cooking interactively by emphasizing unusual flavors in ways that show the connections between their cuisine and the map and bible of their diners. Authenticity is thus a property not of a dish by itself but of the relation between cook, dish, and a diner whose own map and bible is a given. Acknowledging this is not inauthentic but truthful. History shows that culinary insiders have no obligation to preserve their culture "as is," since no culture has ever been preserved in that way. Again, it is worth repeating, expressive authenticity is not about origins but about the commitments people make and what those commitments reveal about their sensibility. There is a reason why tomato sauces marry nicely with pasta and why a tomato served with olive oil and basil is heavenly. Tomatoes may not be originally Italian, but Italians have done wonderful things with tomatoes. They committed themselves to tomatoes, discovering how they resonate with their local ingredients, and now there is a certain way with tomatoes that is uniquely Italian.

So should we just throw out the food rules that are invoked so often as markers of authenticity? I think not. Food rules must be respected because they set the table for innovation—they define the standards that innovation must meet. Food rules say, "If you want to violate this tradition it better be good." Without tradition, innovation is just novelty. However, anyone who is just a slave to tradition and rigidly conforms without entertaining new ideas is threatening the conditions that enable the tradition to persist—its ability to be affected. The ability to be affected is, after all, what sensibility is. Traditions become great because of their capacity to seamlessly absorb new influences. Tradition and authenticity are not opposed to innovation—they depend on it. No tradition can remain alive if it does not innovate by accepting and transforming influences from abroad.

To be authentic, in this expressive sense, is to relentlessly search for the particular, the original path that links us to our past in a way that illuminates a future. It is to grasp what one cares about, to see the possibilities in one's heritage, and "leap ahead" in the care structure without endless dispersal in the face of external demands. Authenticity is creative appropriation driven by a deep concern for what is appropriated. It means being open for a possibility not yet realized that will transform one's heritage in a distinctive way and reveal one's commitment to that heritage—something that is there but latent and unexpressed. Authenticity begins in openness but takes what is discovered in a way that allows the care structure to advance. Authenticity means owning one's openness to influence.

And so the edible arts, perhaps more so than any other artistic genre, have the capacity to gather the tribes through anchoring identities. But these are identities that gain their power from the differences they assert and assimilate. Flavor maps and bibles don't contain canons or rules; they are fields of problems that come seeded with new and unforeseen directions awaiting an event of creativity to express their potential. In this respect, they are like other maps and bibles (though that is seldom acknowledged by the bible thumpers).

8

THE FUTURE OF TASTE

I have argued that our recently acquired interest in good taste is not merely a preoccupation of the wealthy or a signal of class status but also a response to the production paradigm—the idea that more is always better, growth must be constant, and efficiency is the only measure of worth— that threatens to consume all life. The role of good taste is to carve out a space where the production paradigm is less central. Part of my argument is that some aspects of the food revolution are inconsistent with central features of the production paradigm. The intrinsic value of the pleasures of the table; their capacity to anchor genuine communal bonds; and the values of authenticity, particularity, originality, and the do-it-yourself ethos, all of which are tracked by the notion of food as art, resist the transformation of good taste into a standardized, fungible commodity. However, if the production paradigm has indeed penetrated all aspects of life, co-opting everything from religion to the world of fine art, why think the food revolution can succeed as a form of resistance?

Aesthetics is a double-edged sword. It celebrates particularity and deepens subjectivity while uniting people in a community of taste. But the worry is that the aesthetic standards presupposed by a community of taste can turn out to be just another mechanism for the production paradigm to colonize and regulate individual lives. We only have to look at our digital lives to see how this insidious co-optation works. On Facebook and countless other venues online, communities of autonomous individuals spontaneously arise to share preferences, cultivate differences, and give people multiple ways of establishing their identity and constructing their own subjectivity. But Facebook hosts this activity not because of any moral or aesthetic interest, but because the data on how we construct identities can be sold to advertisers and third parties. Subjectivity takes on the form of a commodity, which is then fed back to us as more content that fixes identity and gradually usurps the hard work of identity formation. We can find anything we want on Amazon, Netflix, or Google. Life online is wholly consumed by what appears to be our tastes, our particularities. Yet our tastes are being ordered by the genres and subgenres that govern Netflix suggestions, the clickbait we are offered as news, and the categories of search terms that Google scrapes from our online presence. Taste and aesthetics online have been monetized. More often than not we act like dutiful subjects obediently clicking on every piece of sponsored content, and describing ourselves in terms of the categories of metadata prescribed by the production paradigm.

The by-now standard critique of contemporary consumerism is that it produces a fragmented world of disconnected choices. We construct identities out of what we choose to buy and act spontaneously on any desire we happen to have with no organizing principle or ultimate aim. The self we build today can be gone tomorrow when fashion changes; what we find attractive today need have no connection to what we found attractive yesterday or what will be adored tomorrow. Anything meaningful is immediately commercialized and spreads like kudzu until its repetition becomes so monotonous and routine that it becomes background noise for the pursuit of what's next. There is no purpose other than consumption itself. We call this freedom of choice.

This critique of meaningless consumption has become so common in some circles it too has settled into the monotonous drone of background messages that have as much impact as public service announcements. But the critical point still stands—the ability to choose between brands is not real freedom if the brands are interchangeable and replaceable. The act of choosing is then arbitrary since what you get with one option you could easily have received from the other. This is why brands spend enormous sums to differentiate themselves through their marketing—but if it's just marketing unsupported by genuine originality, we are dupes, not lovers of freedom. Furthermore, if our choices have no real effect on the world, if they are merely passive reactions to the given, which do no work, require no struggle, and leave no mark, then the world in which we live is no longer ours. The freedom we seek in making a home, in shaping a dwelling, will lack material form, as I argued in chapter 2. The capacity of capitalism to produce bright, shiny, new objects that mine the appearance of creativity and imagination without the substance is truly breathtaking and should not be underestimated. Americans pride themselves on their individuality and slip easily into the rhetoric of freedom, but we are really a nation of conformists caught up in the production paradigm. Is there reason to think the aesthetics of food can somehow escape its grip?

RESISTANCE IS NOT FUTILE

As I have argued in earlier chapters, the Slow Food, do-it-yourself ethos is incompatible with the drive for profits and efficiency and thus is relatively immune to corporate takeover. This ethos of artisanal production and aesthetic consumption occupies a different time and space from the concerns of the boardroom and stock market. The exceptions, of course, are operations such as Whole Foods and Eataly, businesses that capitalize on our craving for good taste. Whether these represent a model of the future of taste or an anomaly I'll leave to the business professors to decide. The food revolution is not antibusiness if the businesses remain responsive to the aesthetic and ethical concerns of their customers.

On the production side, excellent food cannot be conceived in a corporate boardroom where shareholder profits must come first. When consumers demand fresh ingredients with a local connection and menu items that are responsive to changes in local tastes, they throw up barriers to corporate control because they resist the standardization that is necessary to maximize profits. Furthermore, great restaurant cooking is possible only when done on a small scale, because the chef or owner must be close enough to the final product to exert iron-handed control over the kitchen. There is a reason why great restaurants feature someone in authority watching every dish that goes into the dining room. This function cannot be shunted off to an employee with no vested interest in the fate of the business. Even the small chains run by celebrity chefs require him or her to exert direct control over the training and monitoring of satellite operations.

The food movement is about the way food gives pleasure, and it encourages community via a social space at some distance from the influence of big corporations. That distance is part of the point. What ties the movement together is a love of particularity. Michael Pollan reports that for Alice Waters, "it was not politics or ecology that brought her to organic agriculture, but rather the desire to recover a certain taste—one she had experienced as an exchange student in France."[1] Particularity is not about merely having a unique experience. It is about the object of the experience itself, its irreplaceability, the personal connections it enables, and "aura" of place from which it emanates, to borrow a term from Walter Benjamin.

It is this love of particularity that fuels the food revolution and resists the homogenization and standardization that maximizes profit for the production paradigm. If consumers really want particularity and originality, they can find it in the preoccupations of the food revolution. However, it would be a mistake to be too sanguine about the prospects of social change given the resilience and ingenuity of global corporations, and the hard fact that feeding the world may need the economies of scale they enable. Global food and wine businesses have shown some ability to maintain their market share by adding originality and authenticity to their sales portfolio. Especially in the wine business, even large corporate producers strive to maintain their romantic image and advertise their products as more authentic and unique than their competitors. Appellation control and loving references to *terroir*, along with massive investments in tourist experiences that highlight local traditions and culture, keep them in the game, usually with the collaboration of all levels of government and civic associations interested in promoting local business. Every locale with any eye on the future is trying to brand their location with marks of distinction to ground their claims of particularity in the interests of greater profit, and these initiatives are often funded by the corporate sector.

But at least these initiatives can sometimes be influenced by the locals if the politics are right. Local communities engage in debates about too much commercialization, traffic, and how to go about preserving the local flavor. Which flavor to preserve is a highly contested issue, and in some cases this can result in preserving a way of life that resists commodification and the harms of excess development.

The ever-present danger for the corporate sector is that the more we come to value authenticity, originality, and particularity, the less patience we have with the homogenization required for commodity production. If communities start to throw out the fast-food chains in favor of local options, we might have a real revolution on our hands. With all their nostalgia-mongering, the faux-authentic marketing machine might be creating the conditions for its own demise. If global capital is to avoid destroying the particularity that supports their profits, then they must allow local developments that are less than profit maximizing in order to avoid alienating producers who don't appreciate the exploitation of their creativity and customers looking for uniqueness and originality. There is potential for real change here. It is worth noting that despite the apocalyptic warnings of doomsayers there are spaces in capitalism for cultural initiatives to open up new possibilities. There is in fact more revolutionary potential in this search for particularity and authenticity than is generally acknowledged.

MINDFUL EATING

Although a global, technologically robust economy will always tend toward uniformity and the imposition of universal standards, taste can be an opposing force to this trend—but only if it is grounded in particularity, creativity, and imaginative expression that avoids standardization and the categories through which mass consumption operates. I put forward this suggestion as a hypothesis in need of testing: Through a certain kind of mindful eating, through developing an aesthetic perspective in which we are actively engaged in defining for ourselves what is good taste, we need no longer passively accept whatever industrial food the production paradigm puts in front of us. Instead, we refine a sensibility that is original, unique, particular, one of a kind, irreplaceable, and thus resistant to commodification. Furthermore, the focal practice of cooking, with its confrontation with the materiality of the world, releases us from the illusion that this particularity can be achieved through mere passive consumption. As I argued in chapter 2, focal practices such as cooking involve the whole person in a creative engagement with reality in which we strive for an excellence shaped by our individuality.

Such an approach to taste is not the mere enjoyment of flavor. Rather it is the search for specific flavors and textures with their own aura of distinctiveness and memory invoking their own history, customs, and traditions. All genuine beauty in the end particularizes and takes the beautiful out of circulation as a commodity. The pursuit of beauty is inherently to come to know something in its particularity—which is opposed to the homogenization and standardization that characterizes many dimensions of contemporary life. Beautiful food has an even greater capacity for such resistance because of the relentless subjectivity of taste. Although there are aspects of taste that are reasonably objective, we each have unique biological propensities and personal histories that make individual preferences irreducibly subjective and that preclude excessive standardization. The tissue of little things is inherently nonfungible.

Thus, the answer to the question of how the food revolution can resist the stultifying commodification of the production paradigm is that we must strive to fill our lives with a sensibility that continually eludes the homogenizing forces of global capital in general and corporate food in particular. The trick is to see oneself as a non-tool, as someone who can escape the logic of the market by refusing to see oneself as an instrument of wealth creation.

This requires that we see our subjectivity, our desires and personal preferences, as something within our control. But given the pervasiveness of media and the influence of a corporate culture over all aspects of life, learning to resist the blandishments of sophisticated marketing machines requires great discipline and the ability to shape desires so they no longer succumb to the pitch. Self-control is the essential virtue if the food revolution is to have a future.

It is ironic that the social theorist most responsible for articulating the insidiously pervasive influence of social norms over our inner lives was also able to see the way out of the postmodern version of the iron cage. In his last works before his untimely death, the French social theorist Michel Foucault began to advocate techniques, forms of knowledge, and thought processes that could direct how we refine desires and pleasures so they become uniquely ours.[2] This requires that we abjure fabricated needs and attend to the complex factors that shape our desires, analyzing the pursuit of pleasure with careful attention to its effects in specific situations and circumstances. To achieve this thoroughly original, personal style that effectively resists marketing ploys we need to be constantly aware of how actors in each situation we confront use power and leverage knowledge and the ability to construct social norms to shape our personal, aesthetic taste. We need to continuously search the history of human inquiry for techniques and practices that respond to the dangers of contemporary life, and we need to maintain a willingness to experiment and test our actions and practices in order to reimagine how we are related to ourselves and others.

Food and drink are not the only arenas in which we can accomplish these "technologies of the self," but because of their ubiquity in everyday life they may be the most immediately accessible. Taste is the arena of life that is most subjective and personal, where there is less pressure to conform because the immediate effects are largely confined to one's own enjoyment. It is also the part of life over which we have the most individual control and thus, arguably, it is the arena where the resistance to dominant norms and the conceptualization of new ways of living can first take hold. Under such a regime of disciplined attention to aesthetics, art would recapture some of its original meaning not only in the art of cooking but also in the art of growing and making things—a fundamental transformation in our relationship with objects.

In modifying the way we eat and drink and altering the discourses, rituals, and limitations we place on such activities we can reform how we experience pleasure. By modifying the way we experience pleasure we modify our relationships to discourses and norms. There is no general solution to getting off the production paradigm, no alternative form of life we can simply step into—only the disciplined practice of good taste prevents the successful hijacking of our subjectivity.

Perhaps the closest parallel to this idea that is already part of our culture is the practice of mindful eating. Instead of our common habit of plowing through a meal while updating Facebook, the Buddhist spiritual leader Thich Nhat Hanh advocates, in his short book *How to Eat*, that we slow down and tune in to the flavors and textures of our food, note the cascade of colors on the plate, and savor the aromas rising from a hot bowl of soup. Rooted in Buddhism as a supplement to other forms of meditative practice, we are encouraged to pay exquisite attention and learn to relish the sensations of each morsel.

> When we eat we usually think. We can enjoy our eating a lot more if we practice not thinking when we eat. We can just be aware of the food. Sometimes we eat and we're not aware that we're eating. Our mind isn't there. When our mind isn't present, we look but we don't see, we listen but we don't hear, we eat but we don't know the flavor of the food. This is a state of forgetfulness, the lack of mindfulness. To be truly present we have to stop our thinking. This is the secret of success.[3]

Often sold as a way to lose weight, mindful eating has become at least a minor cultural phenomenon, receiving some attention from the press and the medical community. By eating slowly and mindfully we are less distracted by the habits and cravings that encourage us to overeat. We are satisfied with less because we experience the food more intensely and revel in the pleasure it brings. We can enjoy even foods high in calories if we eat less of them, an approach that is more appealing than the restrictive diets that most people have trouble following consistently.

Hanh's approach is not limited to the experience of pleasure but includes a recognition of the wider context in which our eating takes place:

> So in this slice of bread there is sunshine, there is cloud, there is the labor of the farmer, the joy of having flour, and the skill of the baker and then—miraculously!—there is the bread. The whole cosmos has come together so that this piece of bread can be in your hand. You don't need to do a lot of hard work to get this insight. You only need to stop letting your mind carry you away with worrying, thinking, and planning.[4]

Included in that wider context is a moral imperative:

> With each meal, we make choices that help or harm the planet. "What shall I eat today?" is a very deep question. You might want to ask yourself that question every morning. You may find that as you practice mindful eating and begin to look deeply at what you eat and drink, your desire for certain foods may change. Your happiness and that of the Earth are intertwined.

Hahn's volume is a remarkable book that will take you a half hour to read and give a lifetime of enjoyment. In fact, a quote from Hanh sums up what he shares with the food revolution: "A few years ago, I asked some children, 'What is the purpose of eating breakfast?' One boy replied, 'To get energy for the day.' Another said, 'The purpose of eating breakfast is to eat breakfast.' I think the second child is more correct. The purpose of eating is to eat."[5] That is a succinct account of what it means to exit from the control of instrumental reason.

Hanh's approach to mindful eating is commendable and certainly in the right direction. But I have some reservations. First, mindful eating is often sold for its instrumental virtue as a means of losing weight. No doubt it fills a great social need and its potential as a method of losing weight will make many lives better. But if losing weight is the primary motivation, it returns eating to the realm of the instrumental, a means to an end, and not something to be enjoyed in itself. The danger is that this can be thoroughly co-opted by the efficiency experts, such as the inventers of the new product Soylent, who strive to put all our nutritional needs in a drink so we no longer have to eat at all. This is the production paradigm on steroids. The weight loss dimension must be understood as a happy side effect of simply enjoying our food more, lest we lose our grip on what is important.

Second, when Hanh asserts that we can see the farmer or the land in a grain of rice or slice of bread, he seems to have in mind a generic farmer or a generic piece of land. Yet it is a particular farmer and a particular piece of land that yields the distinctiveness of artisanal products, and that distinctiveness is part of the pleasure we get from food. It would seem that to get all the enjoyment from food that is available to us we sometimes must come to understand the origin of something, the authenticity of its production, and how that authenticity influences flavor. Hanh continually invokes the importance of not thinking when practicing mindful eating. However, the ability to know where something comes from, to discriminate its subtleties, to note where it fits with other things of that type, and to find enjoyment in all of that, is not just a matter of passive tasting. As I argued in chapter 5, flavor is a complex idea that requires extensive cognitive resources—in other words, thinking. Mindful eating cannot require the absence of thought. What Hanh seems to advocate is when we eat to stop thinking about something other than food—no worrying about the future, or obsessing over a problem at work, or pondering what one will do after the meal. Indeed. The purpose of eating is eating. To be fully present at every moment is surely a good thing. But it is not incompatible with thinking and in fact requires thinking if the richness of each moment is to be realized.

Furthermore, it is not obvious to what degree mindful eating, as described by Hanh, is a full-blown aesthetic experience. The nature of aesthetic experience has been endlessly debated by philosophers, and this is not the place to rehearse the blow-by-blow. But, at the very least, an aesthetic experience involves conscious, concentrated attention that is aware of itself as a heightened perceptual experience and that involves some sort of appreciation. This seems to be precisely what Hanh is after; thus, it is clear that mindful eating is at least a rudimentary form of aesthetic experience. Furthermore, the practice of aesthetic appreciation requires activity that strives to sharpen our perception of an object. As Hanh describes mindful eating, it requires self-discipline and practice to be able to quell the constant intrusion of distracting influences—concentration must be learned just as aesthetic attention must be cultivated in order to sharpen our perceptions.

But if our goal is to derive from these objects of perception—in the case we are considering, the food we eat—the richest experience they have to offer, then we must consider not just simple ingredients but also their interaction with other ingredients and how they harmonize or produce interesting contrasts, the influence of cooking practices on the taste of things, and the relationship between what we taste, where it comes from, who conceived and prepared the food, and how we think about what we taste. Here it is not at all obvious that Hanh will follow, because it seems there is much thinking to be done. My worry is that if we understand mindful eating only as described in *How to Eat*, it can too easily fall back into the realm of the normative and habitual. If our aim is to maximize enjoyment, we need to avoid the inevitable extinction of enjoyment that comes from too much of the same. How long can simple awareness fascinate?

There are clear and relevant differences between the exquisitely discriminated taste of a tangerine, a mindful awareness of the subtleties of a combo meal at McDonald's, and thoughtful attention to a superlative dinner with fine wine at one our fine dining establishments. Does Hanh recognize and value the difference? If not, mindful eating lacks key features of aesthetic awareness.

In the end, the goal of the kind of eating I advocate and that the food revolution is aiming at is to open up a domain of extraordinary beauty to be most fully and completely enjoyed. Is that the aim of Hanh's version of mindful eating? Here is a description of mindfulness by a Buddhist monk and scholar:

> The mind is deliberately kept at the level of *bare attention*, a detached observation of what is happening within us and around us in the present moment. In the practice of right mindfulness the mind is trained to remain in the present, open, quiet, and alert, contemplating the present event. All judgments and interpretations have to be suspended, or if they occur, just registered and dropped. . . . To practice mindfulness is thus a matter not so much of doing but of undoing: not

thinking, not judging, not associating, not planning, not imagining, not wishing. All these "doings" of ours are modes of interference, ways the mind manipulates experience and tries to establish its dominance.[6]

Aesthetic attention, by contrast, is not merely "bare attention"; it need not be detached, although some philosophers insist it must be disinterested, and certainly it does not preclude judging, associating, or imagining. Again, it seems mindful eating is a rudimentary aesthetic experience but not one that contains the richness of a fully realized aesthetic. Lying behind the practice of mindful eating, as Hanh conceives of it, is the practice of Buddhism. Mindfulness, with respect to not only eating but all the other activities in which we engage, is a stepping-stone on the path to Enlightenment in the Buddhist conception and involves ultimately the experience of emptying the intellect, the extinction of desire, and the achievement of Nirvana, goals that go well beyond the need to carve out a space in life where beauty replaces productivity. I suspect the degree to which mindful eating falls short of a full-blown aesthetic experience has to do with the commitment to Buddhism, a commitment that, however commendable, is not shared by the gastrophiles who pour into our temples of gastronomy.

Thus, mindful eating is an important development in our eating practices, a close kin to aesthetic eating, and a kind of resistance to the production paradigm that should be welcomed. Despite the differences with "aesthetic eating" it illustrates the kind of eating practice that, should it be widely adopted, has the capacity to transform our relationship to food and the social and political framework that supports the modern food industry. What are the chances of it being widely adopted? I have no crystal ball, but all it asks us to do is enjoy our food. How hard is that?

CONCLUSION

Today we face the threat of global environmental disaster, overproduction, and the swallowing of life by the production paradigm that diminishes the prospects of human flourishing, and the inability of individuals to do much about any of it. This can lead to a kind of despair that supports dark nihilistic visions of a dehumanized future. My response in this book has been to give up on the production paradigm and return to the virtues of ordinary life and ordinary pleasures, the moments of everyday life over which we have some control, which can escape the clutches of the marketers and can be made remarkable merely through disciplined attention. This empowers us to do what we can without despair. If we can learn to discover and appreciate what we already have available, perhaps we will not be so dependent on acquiring new goods that put even more pressure on available resources. The tissue of little things is inherently nonfungible. But it requires care and maintenance. Without such care, the commodifiers and monetizers will strip it of all beauty.

These considerations should not be dismissed as merely nostalgic, as a sentimental lament over a lost way of life. We have no desire to return to the bad old days where resources were scarce, life was hard, bigotries reigned, and individual liberty was just a theory. A wholesale rejection of modern life is not in the cards. Instead, we should be looking for how, within the framework of modern life as it is, we can find ways of resisting the commodification and homogenization of our world via the cultivation of taste.

As David Bosworth has recently argued in his book *The Demise of Virtue in Virtual America*, in America's past, local self-government and agrarian production were supported by the virtues of self-control, self-reliance, hard work, and a sense of community.[7] These virtues have been made superfluous by the triumph of "evangelical mammonism," another name for the production paradigm that combines a religious devotion to the "free market" with a faith in progress and the attractions of passive, thoughtless consumerism. Artisanal food production and consumption can restore modern analogues of these virtues, not through Stoic resolve, but with the frank acknowledgment that Epicurean pleasure is worthy of pursuit when it solidifies meaning and demands of us the full exercise of our capacities.

I doubt that there is any meaning to life beyond the full experience of it, and that requires the maximum enrichment of our everyday activities. All objects we encounter have a kind of eloquence about them that we are obliged to recognize if we seek this enrichment. Our food is no exception; indeed, food may be the most readily available source of this eloquence, since the enjoyment of food is so accessible to us—all you have to do is eat with full awareness, a capacity we all possess if we learn to taste.

NOTES

INTRODUCTION

1. Sylvester Graham, *A Lecture to Young Men on Chastity: Intended Also for the Serious Consideration of Parents and Guardians* (Boston: G.W. Light, 1839), 169.

2. Harvey Levenstein, *Revolution at the Table: The Transformation of the American Diet* (New York: Oxford University Press, 1988), 210.

3. John Ikerd, "The Local Food and Family Farm Revival," University of Missouri, John Ikerd papers, accessed April 2, 2015, http://web.missouri.edu/ikerdj/papers/Mississippi%20--%20Food-Farm%20Revival.htm#_edn18.

4. Steve Martinez et al., *Local Food Systems: Concepts, Impacts, and Issues*, ERR 97, U.S. Department of Agriculture, Economic Research Service, May 2010, accessed April 2, 2015, http://www.ers.usda.gov/media/122868/err97_1_.pdf.

5. John Ikerd, "Local Food: Revolution and Reality," University of Missouri, John Ikerd papers, accessed April 2, 2015, http://web.missouri.edu/ikerdj/papers/Indiana%20--%20Food%20Revolution.htm.

6. Andrea Hsu, "The U.S Is a Spicier Nation (Literally) since 1970s," National Public Radio, July 30, 2010, http://www.npr.org/templates/story/story.php?storyId=128852866.

7. Specialty Food Association, "State of the Industry 2014," accessed April 10, 2015, https://www.specialtyfood.com/news/article/state-industry-14/.

8. Leslie Brenner, *American Appetite: The Coming of Age of a National Cuisine* (New York: Perennial Books, 1999), 25.

9. Quotations are from David Kamp, *The United States of Arugula* (New York: Broadway, 2006), Kindle edition, chapter 5. Kamp's book is an accessible and entertaining account of the history of the food revolution.

1. WE LIVE FROM GOOD SOUP

1. David Linden, *The Compass of Pleasure: How Our Brains Make Fatty Foods, Orgasm, Exercise, Marijuana, Generosity, Vodka, Learning, and Gambling Feel So Good* (New York: Viking Press, 2011), 3.

2. See Linden, *The Compass of Pleasure*, for an extensive discussion of how addiction differs from the ordinary pursuit of pleasure.

3. The phrase "we live from good soup" is from the Lithuanian philosopher Emmanuel Levinas. The phrase is embedded in a paragraph asserting that we don't represent soup, or air, light, spectacles, sleep, work, or ideas, as something separable from life. We live from them—they make representation possible but cannot themselves be fully represented. Levinas is not responsible for how I am using the phrase, although I think my meaning is not entirely divorced from his. See Emmanuel Levinas, *Totality and Infinity: An Essay on Exteriority* (Pittsburgh: Duquesne University Press), 110.

4. Levinas, *Totality and Infinity*, 133. It should be mentioned that Levinas was no hedonist. Although the self is always bound up in its pursuit of satisfaction, there is, as a matter of equal salience, the face of the other—the suffering other person whose plight disrupts any self-satisfaction.

5. As noted above, pleasure plays a functional role in our neurophysiology as a reinforcement mechanism. But, phenomenologically speaking, we experience pleasure as a surplus, as having intrinsic value.

6. Adam Gopnik, *The Table Come First: Family, France, and the Meaning of Food* (New York: Knopf, 2011), 9.

7. I should note, to avoid misunderstanding, that I am not endorsing the baleful consequences on the environment of this sense of dominion over nature. I'm only pointing to its existence.

8. Jean Jacques Rousseau, *Emile* (New York: Basic Books, 1979), bk III.

9. For a fascinating and much more comprehensive study of the various moral virtues associated with the culture of the table, see Julian Baggini, *The Virtues of the Table: How to Eat and Think* (London: Granta Publications, 2014).

10. Gopnik, *The Table Comes First*, 39.

2. WHY FOOD? WHY NOW?

1. The social theorist most responsible for articulating this "loss of the real" is Jean Baudrillard, whose many books trace the emergence of a global communication system in which we are unable to distinguish reality from its simulation—what is real and what is fiction are woven together and cannot be pried apart through analysis. See Jean Baudrillard, "Simulacra and Simulations," in *Selected Writings*, ed. Mark Poster (Stanford, CA: Stanford University Press, 1988).

2. The view that this form of reason threatens to colonize all aspects of modern life has been with us throughout much of modern intellectual history. Luminaries from Rousseau to Heidegger to Foucault have argued that when taken too far, this is a dangerous form of thinking that threatens to dehumanize life.

3. The question of why instrumental reason and the production paradigm have come to dominate modern life is beyond the scope of this book. For a recent attempt to grapple with this issue, see David Bosworth, *The Demise of Virtue in Virtual America: The Moral Origins of the Great Recession* (Eugene, OR: Front Porch Republic Books, 2014). Bosworth argues that what he calls "evangelical mammonism" is the result of a blind-faith in progress wedded to a religious belief in the pursuit of profit.

4. See Michael Pollan, *In Defense of Food: An Eater's Manifesto* (New York: Penguin Books, 2008).

5. For a philosophical discussion of this understanding of technology, see Martin Heidegger, *The Question Concerning Technology and Other Essays* (New York: Harper Torchbooks, 1982).

6. For a comprehensive account of the political context of the Slow Food movement, see Allison Leitch, "Slow Food and the Politics of Pork Fat," *Ethnos* 68, no. 4 (December 2003): 437–62.

7. From the original Slow Food Manifesto, quoted in Leitch, "Slow Food and the Politics of Pork Fat," 454.

8. From an interview with Petrini, quoted in Leitch, "Slow Food and the Politics of Pork Fat," 455.

9. See Albert Borgmann, *Technology and the Character of Contemporary Life: A Philosophical Inquiry* (Chicago: University of Chicago Press, 1984).

10. Wendell Berry, "The Pleasures of Eating," in *What Are People For?* (San Francisco: North Point Press, 1990), available online at Center for Ecoliteracy, accessed April 21, 2015, http://www.ecoliteracy.org/essays/pleasures-eating.

3. GATHERING THE TRIBES

1. Marcella Hazan, *Amarcord: Marcella Remembers* (New York: Gotham, 2009), 153.

2. This conception of the role and function of art owes a great deal to the views of Martin Heidegger. See especially his essay "On the Origin of the Work of Art" in Heidegger, *Poetry, Language, and Thought* (New York: Harper, 2013).

3. The relationship between restaurant chefs and home cooks will be discussed in more detail in chapter 7. Suffice it to say here that despite obvious differences in training and resources, both aim to make the ordinary extraordinary.

4. The claim that the edible arts take food traditions as their subject matter will be addressed in detail in chapter 7.

5. See chapter 2 for more discussion of the Slow Food movement.

6. For a skeptical view of locavorism as a solution to environmental problems, see James E. McWilliams, *Just Food: Where Locavores Get It Wrong and How We Can Truly Eat Responsibly* (New York: Back Bay Books, 2010).

7. Philosophers should note that by "intrinsic" I do not mean that an aesthetic object has value solely in terms of its intrinsic properties or that it has value independent of the valuation of valuers. "Intrinsic," as I am using the term, simply means noninstrumental.

8. Jacques Rancière, *Disagreement: Politics and Philosophy* (Minneapolis: University of Minnesota Press, 1998), 26.

9. See Jacques Rancière, *Dissensus: On Politics and Aesthetics* (London: Bloomsbury Academic, 2010).

10. The traditions of many other cultures are equally worthy. I use Italian cuisine only as one example among others.

4. FROM PLEASURE TO BEAUTY

1. Quotations are from Steve Poole, "Let's Start the Foodie Backlash," *Guardian*, September 28, 2012, http://www.theguardian.com/books/2012/sep/28/lets-start-foodie-backlash.

2. For a notable exception to this dismissive attitude, see Julian Baggini, *The Virtues of the Table: How to Eat and Think* (London: Granta Press, 2014), 222–33. Baggini's treatment is brief but sympathetic.

3. See Pierre Bourdieu, *Distinction: A Social Critique of the Judgment of Taste* (Cambridge, MA: Harvard University Press, 1984).

4. Nathan Myhrvold, "The Art in Gastronomy: A Modernist Perspective," *Gastronomica* 11 (Spring 2011).

5. Aside from a few notable exceptions, when matters of gustatory taste have been mentioned in the history of philosophy, they have been dismissed as unworthy of extended discussion, and they have never been considered candidates for fine art. In contemporary philosophy, the most vociferous skeptical view is advanced by Roger Scruton, "The Philosophy of Wine," in *Questions of Taste*, ed. Barry C. Smith (New York: Oxford University Press, 2007), 5.

6. Timothy Schroeder, *Three Faces of Desire* (Oxford: Oxford University Press, 2004), Kindle edition. I should mention that nothing in Schroeder's account of desire conflicts with the idea of surplus pleasure developed in chapter 1. I can satisfy a desire without having experienced that desire as a lack or need.

7. William Shakespeare, "Sonnet 116," *Shakespeare's Sonnets*, accessed May 29, 2015, http://www.shakespeares-sonnets.com/sonnet/116.

8. Therry Theise, *Reading between the Wines* (Berkeley: University of California Press, 2011), 34.

9. The role of wonder as a key element of aesthetic response has been much neglected. It has recently received attention from Jesse Prinz in this blog post. Jesse Prinz, "Wonder Works: Renovating Romanticism about Art," *Aesthetics for Birds*, accessed March 29, 2015, http://www.aestheticsforbirds.com/2013/08/wonder-works-renovating-romanticism.html.

10. Elizabeth Telfer, *Food for Thought* (New York: Routledge, 1996), 59–60.

11. Frank Sibley, "Tastes, Smells, and Aesthetics," in Sibley, *Approach to Aesthetics*, ed. J. Benson, B. Redfern, and J. Cox (Oxford: Oxford University Press, 2006), 249.

12. Charles Fernyhough, "The Story of the Self," *Guardian*, January 13, 2012, accessed April 10, 2015, http://www.theguardian.com/lifeandstyle/2012/jan/13/our-memories-tell-our-story.

13. Fernyhough, "The Story of the Self."

14. Leah Mennies, "Flaming Powders and Booze-Soaked Pineapple: What You Missed at Grant Achatz's Harvard Lecture," *Boston Magazine*, April 4, 2011, accessed April 10, 2015, http://www.bostonmagazine.com/restaurants/blog/2011/10/04/flaming-powders-booze-soaked-pineapple-missed-grant-achatzs-harvard-lecture/.

15. The issue of whether a musical work must cause emotion in the listener in order to express emotion is a vexed question for which there is little agreement among philosophers. For a thorough discussion of this issue, see Jennifer Robinson, "The Expression and Arousal of Emotion in Music," *Journal of Aesthetics and Art Criticism* 52, no. 1 (Winter 1994). Robinson endorses the view that the ability of music to express emotion at least in part requires the ability of music to

directly cause certain feeling states in the listener. It is that analysis that I presuppose here.

16. Matt Goulding, "Table for One," *Gastronomica* 12 (Summer 2012): 24.

17. Kent Bach, "Knowledge, Wine, and Taste: What Good Is Knowledge (in Enjoying Wine)?" In *Questions of Taste: The Philosophy of Wine*, ed. Barry Smith (New York: Oxford University Press, 2007), 21.

18. Alexander Nehamas, *Only a Promise of Happiness: The Place of Beauty in a World of Art* (Princeton, NJ: Princeton University Press, 2007).

19. Nehamas, *Only the Promise of Happiness*, 85.

20. Nehamas, *Only the Promise of Happiness*, 77.

21. It should be obvious that casual uses of the term "beauty" are not what Nehamas has in mind if they are simply referring to attractiveness or being pleasant. There are beautiful sunsets, but they are not all beautiful—only those sunsets that are uniquely attractive, awe-inspiring, and that draw us into taking an interest in sunsets would count.

5. HOW TO READ A MEAL

1. William Deresiewicz, "A Matter of Taste?" *New York Times*, October 26, 2012, accessed May 29, 2015, http://www.nytimes.com/2012/10/28/opinion/sunday/how-food-replaced-art-as-high-culture.html?_r=0.

2. Carolyn Korsmeyer, *Making Sense of Taste: Food and Philosophy* (Ithaca, NY: Cornell University Press, 1999), 141. Korsmeyer persuasively argues that food is worthy of serious aesthetic and philosophical attention. Her book has done yeoman work in setting aside the more superficial objections to food as art. Thus, I do not address these arguments here.

3. María Lugones, "Playfulness, 'World-Traveling' and Loving Perception," *Hypatia* 2, no. 2 (Summer 1987): 3–19.

4. Jennifer Ianollo, "Food and Sensuality: A Perfect Pairing," in *Food and Philosophy: Eat, Think, and Be Merry*, ed. F. Allhof and D. Monroe (Hoboken, NJ: Wiley Blackwell, 2007).

5. This data is from Hal Herzog, "84% of Vegetarians and Vegans Return to Meat. Why?" *Psychology Today*, accessed May 29, 2015, https://www.psychologytoday.com/blog/animals-and-us/201412/84-vegetarians-and-vegans-return-meat-why.

6. Exemplification is to be distinguished from denotation, in which symbols refer but do not possess the property to which they refer. See Nelson Goodman, *Languages of Art: An Approach to a Theory of Symbols* (Indianapolis, IN: Hackett, 1976).

6. CAN TUNA CASSEROLE BE
A WORK OF ART?

1. For more discussion of symbols and exemplification, see chapter 5.

2. Ferran Adrià, Juli Soler, and Albert Adrià, *El Bulli, 1994–1997* (New York: Ecco, 1996), 208.

3. Jean-Francois Revel, *Culture and Cuisine: A Journey through the History of Food*, translated from the French by Helen R. Lane (Garden City, NY: Doubleday, 1982), 22.

4. Thomas Leddy, *The Extraordinary in the Ordinary: The Aesthetics of Everyday Life* (Peterborough, ON: Broadview Press, 2012), 121.

5. Leddy, *The Extraordinary in the Ordinary*, 121.

6. Leddy, *The Extraordinary in the Ordinary*, 116–17.

7. HABITS AND HERESIES

1. Jeffrey M. Pilcher, *Planet Taco: A Global History of Mexican Food* (New York: Oxford University Press, 2012).

2. I borrow this term from Denis Dutton, "Authenticity in Art," in *The Oxford Handbook of Aesthetics*, ed. Jerrold Levinson (New York: Oxford University Press, 2003).

3. For an in-depth discussion of this issue, see Joel Rudinow, "Race, Ethnicity, Expressive Authenticity: Can White People Sing the Blues?" *Journal of Aesthetics and Art Criticism* 52, no. 1, The Philosophy of Music (Winter 1994): 127–37.

8. THE FUTURE OF TASTE

1. Michael Pollan, "The Food Movement Rising," *New York Review of Books*, June 20, 2010, accessed May 30, 2015, http://www.nybooks.com/articles/archives/2010/jun/10/food-movement-rising/.

2. See especially the following books by Michel Foucault: *The History of Sexuality, vol. 3: The Care of the Self*, trans. Robert Hurley (New York: Vintage Books, 1988); *The History of Sexuality, vol. 2: The Use of Pleasure*, trans. Robert Hurley (New York: Vintage Books, 1990); *The Hermeneutics of the Subject: Lectures at the Collège de France, 1981–1982*, trans. Graham Burchell (New York: Palgrave Macmillan, 2005); and *The Government of Self and Oth-*

ers: Lectures at the Collège de France, 1982–1983, trans. Graham Burchell (New York: Palgrave Macmillan, 2010).

3. Thich Nhat Hanh, *How to Eat* (Berkeley, CA: Parallax Press, 2014), Kindle edition.

4. Hanh, *How to Eat.*

5. Hanh, *How to Eat.*

6. Bhikkhu Bodhi, *The Noble Eightfold Path: The Way to the End of Suffering* (Onalaska, WA: BPS Pariyatta, 1994), 76.

7. David Bosworth, *The Demise of Virtue in Virtual America: The Moral Origins of the Great Recession* (Eugene, OR: Front Porch Republic Books, 2014).

INDEX

ABOUT THE AUTHOR

Dwight Furrow is professor of philosophy at San Diego Mesa College in San Diego, California. He received his PhD in philosophy from the University of California, Riverside, in 1993 and specializes in the philosophy of food and wine, aesthetics, and ethics. He is also a certified wine specialist earning certification from the Society of Wine Educators and an advanced-level certification from WSET (Wine and Spirits Educational Trust). Professor Furrow is the author of *Edible Arts*, a blog devoted to food and wine aesthetics (http://foodandwineaesthetics.com/), and *Roving Decanter*, a food, wine, and travel blog (http://rovingdecanter.com/), and he is a monthly contributor to *Three Quarks Daily* and *Sommelier Insight*. He is also the author of many professional journal essays, op-ed pieces, and magazine articles in publications such as the *San Diego Union-Tribune*, *Los Angeles Times*, *Humanist*, and *Enterprise Virginia*. His books include *Reviving the Left: The Need to Restore Liberal Values in America* (2009), *Ethics: Key Concepts in Philosophy* (2005), and *Against Theory: Continental and Analytic Challenges in Moral Philosophy* (1995). In addition, Furrow is the editor of *Moral Soundings: Readings on the Crisis of Values in Contemporary Life* (2004).